Invitation
to the
Old Testament

Invitation to the Old Testament

A Catholic Approach to the Hebrew Scriptures

Alice Camille

ACTA

ASSISTING CHRISTIANS TO ACT

PUBLICATIONS

Invitation to the New Testament
A Catholic Approach to the Christian Scriptures
by Alice Camille

Editing by Kass Dotterweich
Cover design by Tom A. Wright
Cover art by Jean Morman Unsworth
Typesetting by Desktop Edit Shop, Inc.

Scripture quotations are from the *New Revised Standard Version* of the Bible, copyright © 1989 by the Division of Christian Education of the National Council of the Churches of Christ in the USA. All rights reserved. Used by permission.

Quotations from the Second Vatican Council documents are from *Vatican Council II: The Conciliar and Post Conciliar Documents, Study Edition.* Ed. Austin Flannery, OP (Northport, NY: Costello Publishing Co., 1987).

Quotations from the *Catechism* are from the *Catechism of the Catholic Church* (Liguori, MO: Liguori Publications, 1994).

Published by: ACTA Publications
Assisting Christians To Act
4848 N. Clark Street
Chicago, IL 60640-4711
800-397-2282
www.actapublications.com

Library of Congress Catalog number: 2004110461
ISBN: 0-87946-271-X
Printed in the United States of America
Year 10 09 08 07 06 05 04
Printing 10 9 8 7 6 5 4 3 2 1

Contents

Dedication

With gratitude to Jonathan Tenney,
wisdom teacher and friend,
who talked me into freedom

Surrendering to the Story

I don't like to be late for a movie. If I take my seat after the story has begun, inevitably the questions multiply in my mind: Who is this guy? What does this woman want? How did they get into this situation? Why should I care about what happens to them? Sooner or later, no matter how much I've missed, I manage to fill in the blanks through guesswork. But the best way to surrender to a story is to be there for the very first frame and to take the same journey the characters take, all the way to the bitter or glorious ending.

I suppose that's why I decided to read the Bible when I had finished college. As a newly graduated English major, it was the first time in years there wasn't something I *had* to be reading. And frankly, because my degree was in English, there wasn't a howling industry demand for my services. With time on my hands and a desire to hear the story once and for all from start to finish, I decided to read Scripture for a half hour every morning. The original idea was to cover three chapters a day, but things didn't always work out that way. Some chapters flowed together in one smooth line of narrative, and others were discreet stories, worth savoring on their own. Some sections of the Bible were easy to take in—say, half a dozen psalms in one morning. Other sections—like a mere three verses from the prophecies of Isaiah—were enough to blow my mind for the day. Little by little, it dawned on me that I'd had it all wrong about the Bible. It wasn't some huge, sprawling book about God as I'd imagined. Instead, it was lots of little books clustered around a revolving cast of characters who understood themselves to be, in a fundamental way, the people of God.

As a practicing Catholic with twelve years of parochial school behind me, I was surprised at how many pieces of the story I didn't know. Who the heck was Tobit? Whatever happened to the great kings of Israel? What made the prophet Jeremiah so morose? How did Saint Paul, who never followed Jesus before the crucifixion, become the greatest apostle?

One of the reasons Catholics may find parts of the Bible wholly unfamiliar is because of the way we are used to hearing Scripture read in church. The *lectionary*, which is the book of readings used at Mass, is set up in a crosshatch style with a "plaid" of cycles that repeats every three years on Sundays and every two years on weekdays—and remains the same each year for certain feasts. During a particular season, there may be a more or less continuous reading of one book from Mass to Mass —for example, we hear the Acts of the Apostles during the seven weeks of Easter—but this is by no means comprehensive. And there is little attempt made to cover the whole Bible in any linear sense from Genesis to Exodus and so on. The readings we hear are selections from a far larger text, at times edited significantly to make them "read" better in short sections. All of this makes the story line of the Bible obscure to the person who encounters Scripture primarily on Sunday mornings.

The truth is, the lectionary is not at the service of the story of Scripture; it was compiled to serve the church calendar. In our worship space, we enter an alternative timeline to the normal ticking of our clocks and the squares on our calendars. Chronological time, where we live and move and do our laundry, is about the here and now. It's about the stuff we do to ensure our next meal and secure a space to take our rest. Clock time is geared to the present; no one ever asks "What time *was* it?" or "What time *will it be*?" but only "What time *is* it?"

What the church participates in during the liturgical year, however, is different. Liturgical time tunes us into eternity, where cycles of birthing and living and suffering and dying and being redeemed are happening in one grand "now" of God's perspective. Being outside of the limiting effects of time and space, God experiences the original creation of the world, as well as the new creation to come, unconstrained by concepts like "past" and "future." So if our linear minds are disoriented by the non-linear movement of the biblical story we engage in liturgical time, that's not surprising or unintended. The goal of the lectionary's organization is not to present history but to give witness to salvation! And as you might expect, the story of salvation does not travel from Point A to Point B as we do. Instead it moves, as theologian Teilhard de Chardin put it, in an outwardly expanding spiral of grace from the Alpha to the Omega point—both of which are God.

All of this is to say that relying on Sunday attendance for our sole understanding of the story line of Scripture is going to be self-defeating. Those who are interested in knowing the story of the Bible will be forced to do something really radical: to actually read it. Those of us who count perusing the television guide as nightly reading will find this idea intimidating. But it's worth taking up the challenge and, unlike television, it could save your life.

Perhaps you have already come to the conclusion that the Bible is a story that concerns you personally, because you too are among the people of God. What does it mean to claim this identity? What does God's story have to do with yours? What does your life have in common with the saints and sinners who inhabit Scripture? How are you being called to participate in salvation history—yes, you—and how will you choose to answer that specific and deeply personal call?

The answers to these questions may be encountered in the Bible, but that's not to say the Bible is a book of answers. The Bible is most profoundly the story of a community of faith, waiting for us to join its story with ours. It would not be off the mark to consider your life as a living text for the next book of the New Testament yet to be written. What will your book be called, and what will be its message? What is God saying to the world by your coming into being as a unique and irreplaceable creation?

You may want to keep these questions in mind as you engage the Scriptures. This book is organized to serve as a guide to that part of the Bible most Christians know as the Old Testament. To the Jewish community that produced these texts in the sweat and toil of their experience, there is, properly speaking, no "new" testament. The books in the first section of our

Bible represent the Jewish *canon*, the complete and authoritative text for Judaism. Since we are about to enter an essentially Jewish story, we'll be using the term "Hebrew Scriptures" interchangeably with the Christian designation "Old Testament." This *testament* (a word meaning "promise" or "covenant") is actually many testaments of individual moments of connection between God and human beings. The Hebrew story contains the great themes of human experience—love and loss, sinning and saving, despair and hope—and demonstrates how humans have responded, one by one, to the invitation to enter into a profound and intimate relationship with the One who is our source and our destiny.

You will notice that each chapter in this book includes reference to the biblical books discussed in that particular chapter. This is not to say that you *must* read those books before reading the chapter; it certainly wouldn't hurt if you did. Others may prefer to read the Scriptures discussed after reading the survey chapter to gain a little background for the task.

Finally, each chapter closes with discussion questions for personal reflection or group use, as well as a recommended prayer activity. If the word of God finds a place in our hearts, then word becomes flesh once more and "all things are possible," as Scripture reminds us. Otherwise, Bible stories remain dusty old pages about exotic events in faraway lands. If we discover the biblical person lurking within us, however, we can step into this story and write the next chapter with every new decision we make.

Introduction

Getting to Know the Bible

In the beginning, for many of us, the Bible was a really large book with a leather cover and gold edging that was displayed in a prominent place in the family home. It may have had thumb grooves to mark the sections contained within it, and the words of Jesus were often printed in red, to show how special they were. This book also had marvelous full-color pictures of significant events—some glorious, others bloody. From the time we were young, we understood this book to be important. It was different from other heavy volumes around the house—for this book alone was holy. In it, we reverently recorded baptisms, marriages and deaths, and always treated it with respect.

We also never read it.

How did the Bible attain the status of the most revered and least read book in the house? For one thing, Catholics customarily owned the Douay translation of the Bible, an authorized Catholic version that retained the Elizabethan tones of its seventeenth-century translators (similar to the authorized Protestant translation called the King James Version). Since no one has talked like that for centuries, reading the Bible was like sitting down to Shakespeare for the first time. Many of us were too intimated to try.

Another reason the Bible became a holy object rather than a familiar text was because earlier generations of Catholics were taught that the Bible was too complicated to be grasped except by religious professionals. Best to leave the interpretation of the Scriptures to the priests, who could communicate God's mind clearly and simply in the Sunday homily. Four hundred years ago, during the Protestant Reformation, Catholics saw the results of having individuals determine for themselves what the Bible was saying. The splintering of Christianity into denominations of independent thinkers was due in part to such personal interpretations. Maintaining an orthodox understanding of the text became an obvious pastoral necessity. Church unity, after all, was too crucial to risk. And so the reading of the Bible for personal, devotional use was by no means encouraged in Catholic circles.

So What Changed?

Many Catholics were brought up on the phrase, "The Church has always taught...." There was a reassuring certainty in that idea. Being part of a long and unchanging tradition made us feel sure that we weren't buying a pig in a poke when we accepted the Catholic position. But something happened in the 1960s that shook up smug users of that phrase: the Second Vatican Council. It is no surprise to anyone over forty that Vatican II changed our relationship to the Bible as it did our relationship to the Mass, our understanding of the Church, and our sense of responsibility to the outside world.

The new outlook on the Bible was no accident. It stemmed from the research of Scripture scholars in the decades prior to the Council. With the discovery of the Dead Sea Scrolls (1947–1956) and other advancements in Bible scholarship, experts were coming to a new appreciation of how the Bible came to be written. Age-old assumptions about a handful of writers setting down the record were replaced with a new appreciation for how whole communities stood behind the evolution of biblical ideas. Far from being notes scrupulously recorded at the scene by proto-journalists, the narratives in the Bible were more like our own family recollections told and retold before they were ever written down. Many of the stories were not intended as historical accounts at all but were meant to say something more timeless and universal than the bald facts. History is necessarily locked into details of time, place and culture. The truths being passed down in the Bible aimed higher than history, because they were meant for people of every age.

As a new understanding of Scripture emerged in the twentieth century, the Church was challenged to incorporate a more vital sense of the Bible into its preaching and practice. These stories didn't belong on yellowed pages for experts to consult and interpret. Living stories demand a living audience to take them to heart and enflesh them for a new generation. And so, in a signal document issuing from the Second Vatican Council (*Dogmatic Constitution on Divine Revelation*, 1965), Catholics were urged to take up the Bible and develop a thoughtful and contemporary understanding of what happens between the Book of Genesis and the Book of Revelation. The Church "has always venerated the divine Scriptures as she venerated the Body of the Lord," declared the Council (no. 21). Venerating Scripture included an acquaintance with it as intimate as our consumption of the Eucharist. As Saint Jerome had said sixteen centuries earlier: "Ignorance of the Scriptures is ignorance of Christ."

Finding the Right Bible

Before you select a Bible for yourself, go to the religious section of any major bookstore. There you will find as many presentations and translations of Scripture as there are people: Bibles for children, teens, adult study groups, or personal reflection. Some Bibles are styled for "boutique" audiences, such as "women's devotional use" or "those in recovery programs." Peddling God's word has become the search for the niche market. If all of this new packaging leads to more honest encounters with the message of the Bible, it's not a bad thing.

Variety, however, can lead to confusion in selecting a Bible for yourself. The main thing is to find a Bible that is inviting to you and meets your needs. Are you a backpack person? Weight and size may be a consideration. Do you intend to curl up in an easy chair with your Bible? Sturdiness and bulk may be preferred. Are you over forty? Look for the large print version.

When considering translations, the New American Bible (NAB) stands apart for U.S. Catholics because it is closest to the text we use in our worship. The NAB translation was made by Catholic scholars, and many versions contain footnotes that explain how the Church has interpreted these texts. The language is contemporary without sacrificing accuracy. Altogether, the NAB remains the most widely used Catholic Bible.

Other translations may be chosen according to purpose or personal preference. The New Jerusalem Bible, for example, was originally a French translation and is thought by many to be more poetic in its language than the NAB. The New Revised Standard Version (NRSV) is the result of collaboration between scholars across denominational lines. Like many Bibles that seek both a Catholic and Protestant readership, the NRSV includes the so-called *Apocrypha*—those books of the Bible that Protestants have excluded from the canon of their Scriptures. (Catholics call these books *Deuterocanonical*, or "second canon," and integrate them into the Old Testament. Any Bible you settle on should include these disputed books, either in the Old Testament section or in a separate Apocrypha section.) If an ecumenical approach to the Bible appeals to you, or if your study group contains Christians of various denominations, the NRSV may be your best choice.

In the end, you may find the punchy modern dialogue of the Good News Bible (also known as the TEV for Today's English Version) more to your liking. And some will always return to the Douay translation because of its comforting familiarity. The best Bible for you, of course, is the one you will actually read.

Approaching the Hebrew Scriptures
Let's say you've got your Bible in hand and are ready to dig in. The Old Testament looms ahead of you with its forty-six titles (including the Deuterocanonical books). Many people who attempt to read the Bible for the first time by starting at page one and plowing through to the last page do not get very far. That approach works for troopers and diehards, but if you're not in those camps, think instead of natural story sections (our table of contents may help here) and set reasonable goals. Two years of short daily passages or a decade's worth of weekly reading is better than trying to digest the whole Bible in one summer. Relax; there's no rush here. Better to have a life-changing encounter with one verse of Scripture than to read the whole book and not once be personally challenged.

Some people take a linear approach, following each book

8

in order until they've read it through. Others may want to jump around: a book of prophecy followed by a historical book or some psalms, just to keep things varied and interesting. Some even prefer to follow each book of Hebrew Scripture with something from the New Testament. (If you choose this method, you may want to check out *Invitation to the New Testament*, the companion book to this volume.) However you proceed, I recommend that groups or individuals minimally commit to reading Genesis, Exodus and Deuteronomy first, since these books are foundational for everything to come.

Since the Hebrew Scriptures tell a story spanning roughly two thousand years (not counting creation) and the cast of characters rivals anything by Cecil B. De Mille, keeping a notebook handy while you read may be a lifesaver. Write down things that seem curious, or questions that pop into your head while reading. Make note of people or places you want to know more about, or jot down family trees. (E.g., Jacob has twelve sons and a daughter, by four different mothers. Who belongs to whom, and in what order do they appear?) If you are using a study Bible, the answer to common questions will appear in the footnotes. Also, most Bibles have some cross-referencing system to send you to other parts of the Bible where the same story or a similar one is told. The new context often leads to additional insights.

If you buy only one outside resource for your reading, consider a Bible dictionary or concordance—or a reference book like *The New World Dictionary-Concordance to the New American Bible* that serves as both. It's small, cheap, and has a remarkably full list of the people, places and important themes in the Bible in alphabetical order. A list of helpful resources for students of the Bible appears at the end of this book (see Selected Resources in the appendices).

Meaning and Story

Rarely do we come to a story "cold," with no sense of what we're in for. Normally when we pick up a book to read or consider which movie to pop into the player, we've already taken certain factors into consideration. One is subject: Are we in the

9

mood for a love story, or cops and robbers? Another consideration is the genre or literary form: Is this poetry, a play, a novel,
or a musical? Then there's the tone of a work: Will this be com-
edy or drama, thriller or documentary? Even if we don't know
the story line of the book or movie we're considering, we do
have some basic information about what's in store, and we prepare ourselves mentally for the experience according to our
expectations. We might expect, for example, to learn some historically reliable data from a documentary. But we know not to
try building the rocket ship described in a work of science fic-
tion!

In reading the Bible, these same considerations come into
play. A poem may be as true as a biography, but the way each
literary form communicates truth is quite different. Is science or
history the only kind of information we trust, or can philoso-
phy and mythology also tell us something true about human
nature and the quest for integrity? Obviously, we have to adjust
our lens for apprehending truth based on the form in which it
is presented. A story about someone who never lived and takes
part in something that never historically happened still has the
potential for telling us something universally true about our
humanity and what motivates us to fail or succeed.

Gaining an appreciation for how stories communicate
their meaning is essential, especially in the twenty-first century,
when the marvels of science and technology have so thor-
oughly impressed us. In our time, the very meaning of truth has
been narrowed to what can be verified in a lab or crunched
through a computer. Archeological advances have forced oral
tradition to cough up some hard evidence or be discounted. If
we can't find a bone or some pottery fragments to back it up,
the story of a people handed down for centuries may be dismissed as mere legend, not to be taken seriously. Without
George Washington's actual ax in hand, we may doubt his
childhood encounter with the cherry tree. But such a response
misses the point of the story, which is not about Washington or
the fate of a tree but the value of honesty and a sense of responsibility necessary for leadership. Whether or not an ax ever met
bark, this is a true story, full of wisdom and insight.

Christians who approach Scripture with an insistence on its literal and historically verifiable truth are known as *fundamentalists*. A fundamentalist reading of the Bible looks for scientific cues—dates, genealogies, cities and events—and constructs from them a precise view of world history and even the future. Among the concerns of fundamentalism are the science of creation based on the Book of Genesis and the exact sequence of events predicting the end of the world derived from the Book of Revelation. Needless to say, modern biblical scholarship doesn't support such a reading, and Catholic teaching since the time of Pope Pius XII (*Divino Afflante Spiritu*, 1943) encourages an interpretation of Scripture based on an understanding of the decidedly pre-scientific worldview of the people who produced it.

Hebrew Scripture Overview

The stories of the Old Testament were passed down by word of mouth long before anyone thought to write them out. The stories of the *patriarchs*—those famous fellows like Abraham, Isaac and Jacob—took their final form some one thousand years after the events they purport to describe, and it's another five hundred years or so until the written form was compiled. So the idea that the stories of the Hebrew Scriptures are historically precise renderings is unlikely. How accurate are your recollections of a decade ago, much less your grasp of what happened 1,500 years before your lifetime? Early Hebrews had no Internet access or outside source materials to consult for confirmation of the facts. They simply told, with occasional elaborations, the stories that had been handed down to them.

The goal of these stories was not to record world history. History as we know it—the business of fact-gathering and preserving the past in an objective sense—had not yet been invented. Rather, the purpose of these stories was to preserve the identity of a people: *This is who we are, who our people have come to be and why. These are the lessons we've learned, how we behave, the laws we observe, and the God we have come to know through our experiences.* When you think of the stories, values, laws and symbols that keep the American identity fresh for each generation, you get the picture. "Give me liberty or give me death!" may or may not be precisely what Patrick Henry said more than two centuries ago, but the reason we tell the story is to recall what it means and what it may cost to preserve our democracy.

And so we have inherited this fascinating collection of books that comprise the story of the Hebrew people, who knew themselves primarily as God's people. Some of it is written as Rudyard Kipling-style *myth*: How Sin Came into the World; Why We Must Work; Why Men and Women Don't Always Get Along. Other parts are probably rooted in the past, such as genealogies, heroic deeds, and central figures who changed the course of history. Works of prophecy often contain *oracles*, which are sayings the prophets understood to be "from God's mouth to your ear." And other writings represent several genres, like the old folktale about a long-suffering soul named Job that was later expanded into a theological reflection on the meaning of human suffering. As we go through each part of the Hebrew Scriptures in this book, we'll pay attention to the kind of story we're dealing with and listen for its unique truth.

Questions for Reflection and Discussion

1 How have you acquired your knowledge of the Bible: Through personal reading? Church attendance? Watching movies? Being taught in school? Give an example of how the Bible has played a role in the development of your faith.

2. Name five events or people you recall from the Hebrew Scriptures. List them in the order you think they appear. Then try to name the book of the Bible in which that story or person shows up. Check to see how accurate you've been.

3. What is your favorite story from the Old Testament, and why has it been important to you?

4. Name some basic stories, themes, values, laws or symbols of the United States. How do these elements convey our national identity? Name similar elements in the Old Testa-

ment that convey the Hebrew people's sense of identity before God and other nations.

5. Which ideas in this Introduction were particularly new to you? How might they affect your appreciation of the Hebrew Scriptures as you hear or read them in the future?

Prayer Activity

Resolve to make one book of the Hebrew Scriptures your own. To make your selection, browse through several kinds of books to get the feel of what appeals to you: poetry, as in the Psalms or Song of Songs; collections of sayings like Proverbs or Sirach; prophecies like those of Amos or Ezekiel; or narratives like Genesis or Ruth. After choosing your book and reading it through, you may want to pursue a deeper understanding by reading a commentary on it or searching for art renderings of its subject. You may also want to create your own drawing or poem in response to what you have learned.

In the Beginning

If you've ever had a baby, changed jobs, moved to a new city, or survived the first day of school, you know how crucial beginnings can be. A false start can sour a new situation, and a confident beginning can set the pace for all that comes after. That's why authors agonize over the first lines of their books. They know that a strong beginning will attract readers and a weak one may cause readers to pass on the book entirely.

We easily remember bold introductions: "It was the best of times. It was the worst of times" (*A Tale of Two Cities* by Charles Dickens); "How do I love thee? Let me count the ways" (*Sonnet 43* by Elizabeth Barrett Browning); "Call me Ishmael" (*Moby Dick* by Herman Melville); "Because I could not stop for Death—He kindly stopped for me" (Emily Dickinson's poem known by the same name). Even folks who aren't particularly religious probably know that the opening words of the Bible are "In the beginning...." What makes this opening unique is that it refers to the *real* beginning—its intention is to tell us about creation itself.

Because beginnings are crucial, this section will focus on chapters 1-11 of the Book of Genesis, the first book in the Hebrew Scriptures. These stories encompass one of the Bible's major themes: the original goodness of the world and how sin became a parasite within it. But before we examine these stories in detail, it would be good to look at how they are told and who is telling them.

Who Speaks?

If you ask a child with any religious upbringing who wrote the Bible, the answer might well be "God." Both Jews and Christians accept their respective canons as divinely inspired. That's not the same, however, as believing a divine finger wrote them, the way Charlton Heston received the Ten Commandments when he played Moses for the movie. Nor does it mean that God is the one telling the story, as suggested by paintings of Saint Matthew taking dictation for his gospel from an angel. As Catholic teaching expresses it, God employed human beings as "true authors" who used their own faculties and powers to write these works. The Scriptures are "affirmed by the Holy Spirit" and contain "that truth which God, for the sake of our salvation, wished to see confided" (see *Catechism of the Catholic Church*, nos. 106–107). This is a greatly helpful phrase. It opens a wide window for the evolution of our understanding. The question it raises remains: Which truth is God confiding here?

A related question is: Who were these "true authors" who cooperated with God, and under what limitations did they employ their "faculties and powers" at the service of the truth? Our present understanding of authorship was not shared by the ancient world. Today we have copyrights and plagiarism laws to protect the intellectual property of writers. As a culture of individualists, we want personal credit for our work. But in the ancient world, writers regularly attributed their work to a teacher or esteemed authority. To write "as if" you were the prophet Isaiah, for example, in his style and using his themes, was a way of honoring the original prophet and conveying that you agreed with his teachings. This approach was not considered dishonest in a culture that valued communal identity more than individuality.

This is how the first five books of the Bible came to be known as the *Books of Moses*. (They are also known as the *Pentateuch*, which means "five volumes.") Because Moses is the great hero of these books and his story encompasses four of them, it is not unusual that this collection would be credited to him. Moses' death, however, is recorded in the Pentateuch; the idea that he wrote about his own death is therefore more than a little suspect. Scholars now believe these stories existed as oral tradition for centuries before finding their way into the written record in the sixth century B.C.

Several schools of thought are represented in the Pentateuch, each distinguishable by the Hebrew names they use for God and the concerns they express for the community. One group is called the *Yahwists*, because they speak of the God known to them by the unpronounceable four letters YHWH. The God they describe is personally involved with the created world and especially invested in human history. You can see evidence of the Yahwist school in the stories of Noah and Abraham, for example, who speak to God as to an acquaintance.

Scholars identify a second school governed by the *Elohists*. They know God as Elohim, the Most High, a distant and fearful force to be reckoned with. This almighty God can be seen in the stories about Moses and Mt. Sinai, among others.

A third contributor to the Pentateuch is the *Priestly* school. Not surprisingly, these authors are concerned about ritual: the correct way to worship, what sort of liturgy is pleasing to God, what constitutes a holy object. We can hear the Priestly school at work in passages about the proper way to prepare the grain or animal sacrifice.

A fourth source arises from the *Deuteronomists*. Their perspective is lawyerly, obsessed with long lists of rules featured in books like Exodus and Deuteronomy. It can be painfully obvious when we come across a section of the Pentateuch attributed to the Deuteronomists—but it's worth it to hang in there. Laws can provide fascinating insights into the people who created them. Because large sections of the first five books are dedicated to these concerns, another name for the Pentateuch is simply *the Law*.

When reading these books, listen for and try to identify these four voices chiming in to tell the story.

A World Is Born

We live in an age when scientists can watch the birth of a star and describe the forces that culminate in the evolution of new planets. Will there be life on those planets? Will a new Adam and Eve emerge at the tail end of those processes—key players who will tend their distant gardens and make their own choices? Science-fiction writer and Christian apologist C.S. Lewis thought they might. He wrote the novel *Perelandra* about the start of a fresh world in which the first people find all of the old choices waiting for them. Good and evil at once take their positions around the naïve inhabitants of Perelandra. If there is a tempter biding his time in every garden, will a savior also emerge to redeem the future with hope?

The creation story in Genesis does not make predictions about other worlds, but it does illustrate some vital realities in ours. Actually, it's more correct to say that there are *two* creation stories in Genesis: one in the first chapter and another in the second. They represent different strains of the oral tradition that the early compilers of the Genesis collection did not feel compelled to choose between. The fact that there *are* variant stories should be enough to discourage fundamentalist thinking about the origins of the world. No one story claims to tell the definitive history of how it all began, but each imparts general truths about the nature of our place in the scheme of things.

In the first creation story, God brings order out of chaos in neat stages over six days. This order comes largely from the separation of opposite forces: light from darkness, the heavens from the earth, water from dry land, and eventually male from female. These forces are not adversarial but complementary. There is a lovely balance in the world that God declares "good." God creates human beings as the apex of this ordered world. The human beings are the last to arrive in this teeming environment—the only creatures to bear God's image. Male and female are created simultaneously and as equals. Together they are given dominion over the rest of the creatures.

Once we enter chapter two, however, we hear a different narration. Scholars consider this second version of the story to be the older of the two. Here, the first person is created before there is so much as a blade of grass pushing up from the ground. This person, known as *Adam* ("earth person" in Hebrew, formed from the clay), becomes the focal point for the creation that will be fashioned according to his needs. In this barren world God plants a garden just for Adam and transports him to it. Curiously, God chooses to plant two very dangerous trees in the midst of this garden: one is the tree of knowledge of good and evil, which Adam is forbidden to touch. The other, the tree of life, bears no instructions. But to keep Adam away

18

from this second tree, God will remove him from the garden in the end.

In chapter two of Genesis, the order of creation has been rearranged and the role of the female is subordinated to the needs of Adam, which is demonstrated by her secondary origin. Eve is created from Adam's side because no other creature has yet satisfied Adam's desire for companionship. God's breath brought Adam to life; Eve's arrival is a bit of a second thought.

Clearly, the two creation stories are answering different questions about what we are doing here. Chapter one communicates wonder in the amazing perfection of God's world and how plentiful, varied, balanced and good it was intended to be. Chapter two holds the seeds of pessimism, a hierarchy of genders, and the brooding foreknowledge of temptation. Which worldview would prevail?

The Trouble Begins

A fresh start always gives us hope that—*this* time—we are going to get it right. Recently I moved into a new house, and walking through the bare rooms I imagined how perfect my new life here would be. How clean everything was! Not a mark on the walls, no clutter, nothing broken!

Within a few days, however, the marks began to appear, I broke a favorite dish, and clutter loomed in every corner. A fresh start offers the illusion that we can preserve the immaculate first moment and keep the damage of our past behind us. Experience continually reminds us that such perfection is not long for this world.

The story of the first sin ferrets out the root cause of that grim reality. What happened to the perfect world God created? It's pretty clear that God intended good, so the "bad" must come from us. Yet it was God who put the controversial trees in the garden in the first place, not to mention the serpent. (The story says the serpent is the most cunning animal *God had made*.) So the potential for bad exists in the world even before humans choose it. God organized the primordial chaos by separating it into opposites; we can imagine that good and evil were part of that labor of division. God alerted Adam to the danger by forbidding him access to the tree of knowledge. It's as if all the potential for evil inherent in the chaos before creation was sealed up in that one place and might somehow remain there if left undisturbed. But when the serpent makes his pitch and humanity falls for it, the power of chaos is released.

What do we learn from this story? One thing it demonstrates is the precious gift of free will that being made in the image of God gives us. Unlike the animals, we don't survive simply on instinct or at the uncomprehending level of cell division. Instead, we are thinkers and choosers of our way, creators of our destiny. We are not slaves of God or biology. Related to God through the intimacy of that shared image, we are free to grow closer to or move apart from God's will.

The results of the decision to move apart are tremendously sad. In the story of Adam and Eve, we see the ruin that befalls our relationships when we choose alienation over belonging. Initially, the first people hide their vulnerable nakedness from each other. Next, they try to hide from God—and the blame game begins, as the man points to the woman and she to the serpent. These two have forfeited their harmony with nature and will now know the enmity between their offspring and the serpent. The creative power they share with God will now be borne in pain, as in the begetting of children or the production of food from the land. Most of all, the end result of separating from God, the source of life, is mortality.

Even though the first people chose separation, God's care for them is still touchingly evident. God makes leather clothes to protect them and resettles them in a new place. Humanity is not abandoned. God remains vitally invested in us and in what becomes of us.

A Spiral of Separation

I don't remember the first time I told a lie—but I do remember the first time I was caught telling one! After punishing me, my dad said he hoped I would learn a lesson from this experience. The lesson he hoped to teach me, of course, was to tell the truth. What I learned, unhappily, was how to lie better the next time so as not to be caught.

One would think that the awful consequences of the first sin would convince humanity to play it straight from that point on. But sin is "sticky." Once we're caught in its web, struggling against the impulse to sin just makes things that much worse. As Saint Paul would later admit, even when he wanted to do the right thing, he didn't; and when he wanted to resist the bad thing, he couldn't. Sin is a form of chaos let loose into the ordered world that continues to unravel us, bit by bit.

So the children of the first couple inherit the allure of sin. Cain becomes jealous of Abel, and God warns him to master his impulses. He doesn't, and after killing his brother, Cain has the audacity to lie about it, telling God he doesn't know where his brother is. God then pronounces a sentence of restless wandering on him, and Cain fears he too will be killed by anyone who guesses his secret. In response, God puts a mark of protection on the first murderer so that no one should take vengeance into his own hands and strike Cain down. In this way God stays close to the human story even in its dark hours, doing a divine version of damage control on a world veering ever farther from God's will.

Noah and the Promise

Reading Genesis chapters 1 through 6 reminds us of Peter's lament, "How often should I forgive? As many as seven times?" (Matthew 18:21) God clearly gets stuck on the forgiving end of the bargain far more often than we do. Since most of us don't manage to forgive seventy times seven times, we are not surprised when God grows tired of the constant demands on divine mercy as well. God expresses regret and grief for having created humanity at all. As the story goes, if it weren't for Noah, God would have lost faith in humans completely. But Noah is the child born to bring relief—and he does so in a big way. He not only rescues the future of humankind but is given stewardship over the animals. Sound familiar? Noah's family and the contents of the ark become the new creation given a chance to rise above the stickiness of the sinful world. Even God seems to place hope in the fresh start.

21

After the Flood, Noah receives the first recorded *covenant*, or promise, God makes with a mortal. God resolves not to deluge the earth again in this way because "the inclination of the human heart is evil from youth" (Genesis 8:21). Here God acknowledges what theologians would later call *original sin*. Sin is part of the world, and each generation is born into its effects.

This thesis is proven in short order by Noah's son, Ham, who makes sport of his father's hapless first adventure with wine (see Genesis 9:20-22). (Ever wonder why Canaanites get such a bad rap in the Bible? Ham will be the father of a son named Canaan.) Respect for parents is so important in the Hebrew story that it will later become one of ten unbreakable rules of Israelite society. We can see that shortly after God forges a new bond with creation sin is back in full swing. And with the building of the Tower of Babel (see Genesis 11), the disintegration of humanity is all but complete. Call it the curse of nationhood: People are suddenly separated by language and loyalties. We no longer understand each other and therefore see no reason to pull together. The original harmony of creation vanishes under the rubble of alienation.

Will God's promise to remain with us hold, even when we choose every avenue toward self-destruction? The end of chapter eleven in Genesis holds the key to answering that question. That's where we pick up the story next.

Questions for Reflection and Discussion

1. Compose the opening line of your autobiography and explain why this beginning is necessary in telling your story.

2. Consider how your family's story might be told differently from the perspective of your grandparents, parents, siblings, children, and you yourself. How do these shifting perspectives assist in reading the different voices of the Pentateuch?

3. Read the two creation stories in Genesis (chapters one and two). What assumptions does each writer make regarding

the relationship between God and creation? Between the man and the woman? Between humans and the world around them?

4. What is the "bad news" of the story of the Fall? What might be the "good news" of that story? How does this story explain the dynamic of sin as you see it in the world today?

5. Name some ways in which the Hebrew story of the Flood reveals a shift in understanding the relationship between God and humanity.

Prayer Activity

Contemplate the alienation that sin creates (as depicted in Genesis 1–11) between God and humanity; between men and women; between humanity and nature; between family members; between God and creation; between one nation and another. Match these stories to present-day situations that mirror their effects. Consider how these situations challenge you to heal divisions in your life.

Genesis 11:27–50

Promises and Patriarchy

How far back can you trace your family tree? For many of us, the story line blurs beyond a few generations and may have begun in a country other than this one. What happened before that last traceable date may seem lost to us, but the story of the past still plays out its consequences in the present generation. All of us owe a great deal to people whose names we may no longer know.

In the same way, the people whose stories are told in the Bible did not live outside the flow of history and its effect. Although we are tempted to trace the biblical story exclusively through the actions of major characters like Abraham and Moses, we have to acknowledge that humbler people made choices that set the stage for what the primary actors would accomplish. For example, one of the "little people" of salvation history is Abraham's father Terah. Although his story takes up only six verses in chapter 11 of Genesis, what Terah does and doesn't do influences what happens to his more famous son.

Terah was from Babylon. By biblical standards he was a pagan, following the gods of the city of Ur. He had three sons, the youngest of whom died, leaving a child named Lot. Terah's oldest son Abram married Sarai, and the couple remained childless. Only Terah's second son seemed to prosper in Ur, which may be why Terah decided to cut his losses and move away. He determined that life might be better in the land of Canaan. Terah persuaded Abram and Sarai and his grandson Lot to take the long journey with him. But they never made it to Canaan. Halfway there, in Haran of Mesopotamia, the group settled until Terah died.

This is an interesting little story for several reasons. It sets up the forward motion of Abraham, the man who would be the

25

father of nations. It also introduces Canaan as a land of dreams, desirable to attain. It establishes the relationships of characters that will become significant later: orphaned Lot, faithful Abram, and childless but beloved Sarai.

But more than that, this story shows us what happens to dreamers who choose security over the fulfillment of their dreams. Terah talked of going to Canaan, but he never got there. Maybe he got tired; maybe the situation in Haran was attractive; maybe he stopped believing in Canaan; maybe he felt too old to continue the journey. Whatever the reason, Terah dies in Haran and so passes into obscurity. It falls to his restless son, Abram, to become one of the most celebrated figures in the Hebrew story. Because Abram is willing to take up the dream, the man who seemed destined to childlessness becomes the founding father of a people more numerous than the stars in the sky (see Genesis 15:5).

Why Abraham?

Abram, it must be admitted, is no likely candidate for the grand designs of history. Coming from Ur, he did not even know the God who first spoke with him in Mesopotamia. Of course, as the Bible record goes, God hadn't talked personally with any-one since the time of Noah. Yet Abram, seventy-five years old and without heirs, entrusts his fate to One who tells him that he will be the father of a great nation, blessed for all time (see Genesis 12:2). Call it faith or hope against hope, but Abram is willing to follow this unknown "God of the promise" beyond all reason and despite all odds.

Here we see one of the most frequently applied biblical principles: God's favor rests on the unexpected one, the least likely to succeed from the perspective of logic. God is shown to be a bit of a gambler, delighting in long odds. God's ways, as the prophets will assure us later, are not our ways. We tend to count on the "sure thing": strength, position, wealth, numbers. For these reasons we might be tempted to put our money on Lot, who is younger and more likely to produce heirs. Or better yet, we'd bank on Terah's other son back in Ur, already married and established. Old Abram and his aging wife do not seem to be a couple with a future. Why would God choose them?

This is an important question, because the answer offers a glimpse into how God's will operates. The Bible writers assert that God is attracted to two traits: loyalty and the willingness to take a risk. Abram is a prime example of both. He has been married to Sarai for half a century, yet even when their union fails to produce children he does not divorce her or take an additional wife. That kind of loyalty is admirable—to a woman in those days, almost unthinkable. After all, the purpose of marriage was to ensure the future, and clearly there would be no "future" from Abram and Sarai. We are left with the radical proposition that Abram loved his wife and wanted a life with her even more than heirs.

The second quality that seems to attract God—risk-taking—is something Abram demonstrates when he leaves Ur with his father. Uprooting and journey are in his blood. The fact that he agrees to the plan so readily leads us to believe that Abram is fundamentally a gambling man. We'll see this tendency again when he dickers with God over the fate of Sodom and Gomorrah and bargains for the life of Lot and his family.

Why would God admire the qualities of loyalty and risk-taking in humanity? Maybe because these are traits we hold in common with our Maker. God is unfailingly loyal to fallen creation. And the act of creation to begin with was a tremendous gamble of free will and surrendered control. Through the exercise of these traits, Abram demonstrates a spark of what humanity holds deep in its nature: the image of God.

How do you and I employ loyalty and risk-taking as followers of the God of Abram? Are we faithful to God and to those we love, even when they don't "produce" what we had planned or hoped for? Are we willing to sacrifice what we can know and touch for the sake of an unforeseeable future? Do we believe God's promises even when they contradict our experience? We follow a living God who guarantees us life everlasting, yet all we see is death at the end of the trail. Are we willing, like Abram, to journey beyond where logic takes us?

God's Covenant with Abraham

An old Franciscan priest once preached at a local parish about the meaning of *covenant*. "Three things to remember," he intoned heavily. "Covenants are promises. They are unequal. They are bloody." It is helpful to keep these elements in mind as we listen to the sometimes eerie details of biblical covenants. In Genesis 15, God assures Abram that his countless descendents will settle in the land of Canaan. To guarantee it, God proposes a covenant between them, one that involves the sacrifice of five animals, three of them cut in half to form a path through which God will pass. As night falls, Abram goes into a trance and watches as a smoking brazier and flaming torch pass between the carcasses. The covenant is hereby sealed.

What is the meaning of this strange ceremony? Normally, covenants were treaties proposed between a king and his subjects—two parties with unequal power. In the agreement, the king promised protection with his armies and governance by divine favor. In return, the subjects agreed to pay taxes with their goods and promised their loyalty. The deal was sealed in blood to make a singular point: Should either side break the covenant, it would be at the price of blood. Kings were often assassinated or villagers slaughtered for not fulfilling their part of the bargain.

What is curious about the covenant between God and Abram is that God alone walks through the carcasses, which suggests this agreement is rather one-sided. Should the covenant fail, God's blood—not Abram's—is at stake. In chapter 17, however, another version of the covenant story is retained within the tradition. At this time, God gives Abram a new name, *Abraham,* confirming his new calling to be a father of nations at the unlikely age of ninety-nine. After promising land and descendants, God requires Abraham to pledge a sign of the covenant through the males of every generation: circumcision of the foreskin. This time, human blood validates the covenant.

Stories of blood covenants seem strange and primitive today, and no wonder. As far as we can tell, Abraham lived about four thousand years ago, in the Middle Bronze Age—

hardly a modern man of contemporary sensibilities. Still, children who bond as "blood brothers and sisters" by pricking their fingers with a pin display the ancient instinct to seal a pact with blood. Blood is a naturally inspired symbol of life, just as fire is an ancient symbol of divine power, and neither disappears after the time of Abraham. Consider how the sign of blood emerges once more in the "new and everlasting covenant" we celebrate at every Mass and how blood and fire deliver God's life and Spirit to us as Christians. The more we consider Abraham's twilight vigil awaiting the sign of God's promise, the more familiar it becomes. Four thousand years may not be so long ago after all.

Crooked Lines

They say God draws the path of grace with crooked lines, and that is never clearer than in the stories of the *patriarchs*—those men of Genesis lined up from Adam to Joseph. Adam is the original sinner, of course, and the line doesn't get much straighter from there. His son Cain is a murderer; Noah has a problem with wine; Abraham is always looking for a shortcut to God's will; Isaac is feeble; and Jacob is a deceiver whose reputation is so notorious that it remains a joke, even to the time of Jesus, to say how rare it is to find a son of Israel without guile. (*Israel* is another name for Jacob.) Joseph, the last of the official patriarchs, is obnoxiously conceited and vain. Taken together, one imagines that salvation history could have done better in central casting!

But as sinners in our own right, we might be grateful that God chooses from among our kind to propel forward the story of hope. Take Abraham, for instance. God accepted Abraham's remarkable faith in the divine promise "and reckoned it to him as righteousness" (Genesis 15:6), as the story goes. God knows Abraham isn't perfect but accepts his fidelity in place of moral perfection. Abraham reveals his weakness when he lies about Sarai (later Sarah) being his sister rather than his wife in order to save his skin in foreign lands. He loves her, but he isn't above using her! When Sarah comes to him with the idea that her maid Hagar might conceive a child by Abraham to fulfill God's promise, Abraham does not protest, even though he had

29

received no such instruction from God. As Sarah's jealousy of Hagar deepens, Abraham permits his wife to abuse her maid until the pregnant woman is forced to run away.

Perhaps Abraham's most morally ambiguous act is his willingness to slay Isaac to prove his fidelity to God (see Genesis 22). Child sacrifices were not unheard of in that pagan age, and Abraham does not take up the act without great sorrow. Yet everything God has said to him up to this point does not deter him from pursuing what he perceives to be the will of God.

Does God ask Abraham to do this terrible thing, even as a "test"? The way the story is told, the command comes from God, as do many other violent commands within biblical history—generating an image of God that we would find incompatible with the gracious and merciful God we meet in Jesus. But remember, this is a covenant story full of gross inequalities in power: Abraham experiences himself in the grip of the will of a divine being who is still wrapped in mystery; Isaac is likewise mute and resigned before the intentions of his father. Like Isaac, we see the fire of the holocaust and know that blood sacrifice is imminent. Covenant stories will have their bloodletting—but must it be at the expense of human life? Would God ask this of a parent? Is our God this kind of God?

If Scripture were a journal of historical events, we would be forced to answer yes. But because we know that this story was meant as a teaching tool—to reveal to a nation its identity before God—we have room to consider it allegorically. The final answer is more important than Abraham's original perception of it: God surely does *not* want human life to be sacrificed. The angel stays Abraham's hand and the nightmare of loss ends. We may not know what call Abraham was following—divine summons or inner compulsion—but we do know what he learned through this encounter.

Through this event, God's people take a giant step forward in understanding. Their God will not be like the pagan gods who demanded the blood of children in order to ensure the future. Old dictates about who God is and what God wants can no longer be obeyed. The God of Abraham is preparing a new way of liberation and hope.

From Canaan to Egypt

Many of us would be more comfortable taking the journey of faith if we knew for sure where it ends. From here to a promised land? From the present hour to some certain future? If God would issue maps with "You Are Here" circled in red and the destination clearly defined and marked, it would make the business of believing a whole lot easier. Sometimes we think of the Church as a road map of this sort. We "Pass Go" at baptism, gather up our sacraments along the way, and expect to see heaven and an accumulated award somewhere in the vicinity of Park Place. It may be frustrating to us to abandon that idea in favor of biblical journey: a road that is not linear, upon which the journey is the destination. Or as Jesus liked to say, the kingdom we seek is right at hand.

Abraham takes his journey and eventually arrives in the land of promise. But that is by no means the end of the road for the nation God has made of him. His son Isaac marries strong-willed Rebekah who will assist their son Jacob in deceiving his father while cheating his brother Esau of his inheritance (see Genesis 27). (So much for biblical family values!) Jacob the cheater is then in turn cheated by his father-in-law Laban, garnering two wives in place of one, with two concubines to spare. This splintered generation will produce the next one: twelve sons and a daughter, who together cause as much grief to their father as is humanly possible. The hope of this generation arises from Rachel, the wife with the most trouble conceiving and the one who bears the two youngest of Jacob's sons. Her son Joseph is despised by most of his brothers, and it is through his debasement in slavery that the entire family—and the nation they will become—will ultimately be saved.

What do these stories teach us? Obviously they are not guides for moral living. Scripture may be called "the good book," but much of its content describes the immoral choices of people who are far from perfect. A reading of Genesis does not suggest that a brother may kill his brother or a son should deceive his father. A family ought not slaughter a city in recompense for the rape of a sister. And no matter how much you detest a relative, it is not right to sell her or him to a passing

31

band of traders. Those who look to the Bible for role models might well be appalled.

What we do gain from these stories is the understanding that God chooses to enter into personal relationships with flawed human beings, not once but repeatedly, making covenants with folks who do not automatically become better just because God chooses them. God does not prevent their often disastrous choices but does reclaim those choices for divine purposes. God may not intend for Joseph's brothers to sell him into slavery, but God can redeem that choice by transforming an act of destruction into one of salvation. If we look at both Testaments of Scripture, we can see this strategy is one of God's favorite ideas.

Questions for Reflection and Discussion

1 Give an example of choices made by your parents, grandparents, or others that affected the direction of *your* life. Who might be affected by decisions you have made or are making today?

2. God seems to choose the least likely folks to share in the divine favor. Identify someone in your family, community, or on the global scene whom God might be using for divine ends, no matter how unlikely he or she appears.

3. In which relationships and commitments do you demonstrate your loyalty? Under what circumstances do you take risks? How do you see God using those traits in your life to accomplish holy purposes?

4. Consider the idea of covenant as Genesis describes it. How does it relate to your understanding of the Eucharist?

5. List obstacles you have faced on the road of faith: doubt; God's apparent betrayal; your own occasions of sin; injury at the hands of loved ones or the Church. Have any of these difficult hours been "redeemed" for you? How has your faith been strengthened through these difficult times?

Prayer Activity

Trace the journey of your life. You may want to tell the story in terms of your career as it appears on your resume, places you've lived, significant people in your life, or things you've learned. Draw a map of this journey and mark the covenants you've made with God, with others, or perhaps with yourself. Reflect on where your journey may be leading you.

Salvation by Journey

Have you ever been rescued? Has a danger loomed in your life—flood, fire, earthquake, tornado, illness or accident—only to find you on the other side of it, safe and sound? Rescues are often experienced in matters less tangible as well. Think of an occasion when you felt friendless or abandoned and then someone arrived in the nick of time to lift your spirits and confirm that you are loved. Rescues can even be described in spiritual terms. A temptation to do wrong may come your way—to blow off a responsibility; to lie; to seek revenge; to gossip or steal or cheat—and then the will to resist temptation suddenly emerges from within you and you turn away from the precipice of a destructive choice and remain unscathed.

The business of rescue is what salvation is all about. *Salvation* is a churchy word that can seem distant from our experience. Often the concept is used in a specific sense when religious folks ask the question: "Are you saved?" Fundamentalist Christians will answer such a question simply: "Yes. I have accepted Jesus as my personal Lord and Savior." Catholics, however, may feel confused by this way of talking about salvation. We know the sacraments address the effects of sin in our lives and cleanse, heal, reconcile and strengthen us for the journey of faith. But we don't speak of a single instant in our lives when we are "saved" from sin and death once and for all. Instead, Catholics view salvation in two distinct ways: first, as an event Jesus accomplished in his passion, death and resurrection (known as the *Paschal Mystery*); and second, as a process in which we participate our entire lives, choosing or rejecting it as we make our way. Our salvation, as we understand it, is realized in its entirety after death when we enter the kingdom of God in its fullness.

The Bible is often referred to as *salvation history* because it traces the story of God's fabulous rescue of humanity from the consequences of our own choices. From the time we first chose the perilous route away from God, God was preparing the means of our rescue from the corruption of sin and death that would inevitably result. Salvation history demonstrates how incorporating the reality of being saved takes time and recognition on our part. A lifeguard may rescue us from drowning, but if we dash back into the water without learning how to swim, chances are we'll find ourselves in trouble again before too long.

Knowing God by Name

By what name do you address God when you pray? "God," of course, isn't a name; it's more like a job description. In fact, most of the names we use for God describe what God *does* rather than who God *is*.

God is known by many names in the Bible, as we have already seen. And since God is infinite, we can count on discovering many more names for the divine in the course of a lifetime—without exhausting all the possibilities. God was originally known as the Creator, and later variously as the God of Mt. Sinai, the God of the promise, or the God of Abraham. But in the Book of Exodus, the people who have formed a covenant with God come to know the Holy One by several other names. These names come to light through the singular association God forms with a fellow called Moses.

Moses falls into the usual category of Least Likely to Succeed as a Bible Hero, which is another way of saying he makes a perfect candidate for salvation history. Moses was born into a Hebrew family in Egypt, in a generation that no longer remembered the years when Egyptians and Hebrews saw their relationship as mutually beneficial. The Hebrew people had done well in Egypt—too well, in fact. They had become a strong nation within a stronger nation, and therefore they were feared and subjected to slavery.

So Moses was born into a suppressed race. Yet he was also a prince of Egypt due to the timely intervention of five women who rescued his life as an infant. (More on this story in the chapter on "The Women of Salvation History.") Caught between two worlds, Moses' loyalties were divided until the day he saw an Egyptian beating a Hebrew slave. Overcome with passion, he rescues the slave by killing the attacker. When his deed becomes known, he flees the country.

In the desert, Moses again rescues some women who are being mistreated by shepherds. In time he marries into their family and reinvents himself as a simple shepherd. One day while tending the flocks, he encounters a miraculous bush that burns but is not destroyed. In its glow, he encounters the divine presence as "the God of Abraham, the God of Isaac, and the God of Jacob." Before too long, people will be adding "the God of Moses" to that list.

Moses is given a commission: to free God's oppressed people in Egypt. To Moses it seems insufficient to identify the God who makes such an audacious request with a mere tabulation of ancestors. Moses asks for a name, a more intimate proof of the God who sends him. He wants a name to communicate the nature, power and authority of the one who makes this demand of the Pharaoh of Egypt. God gives him a curious reply, which in Hebrew has four letters: YHWH.

YHWH has been interpreted as Yahweh or Jehovah (its later Latin rendering), but the lips of mortals were not meant to pronounce this name lightly. The ancients believed names had power. A child would not have been called "Jasmine" or "Rich" simply because the parents liked the name. A name was understood to shape your destiny or call the future into being. Infants were named according to the hopes or sorrows of their parents. People like Abram and Sarai were often renamed in order to appropriate a new way of life. When God entrusted the divine name to Moses, it was a great pledge indeed. The exact meaning of the name is not known, but it implies pure existence. Many of us know it by the translation: "I Am Who Am." The name of God is so unspeakably holy that many centuries later Jesus will be accused of blasphemy just for saying "I AM."

The God Who Saves

"The God Who Is," the only and true God as we might say, is beyond the power of human language to capture. Every religion has grappled with the perplexity of that truth. How can we talk about God at all, unless we know who God is? It would be fair to say that the whole Bible is aimed at revealing the nature of God. Scripture assists us in entering into that ultimate relationship the same way we enter into any other: through knowledge and experience.

No one in the Hebrew Scriptures has a more intimate experience of God than Moses. He receives the name of God and bears it reverently back to Egypt. There, by the power of that name, he wrestles against the might of Pharaoh's kingdom. Ten terrible plagues cripple the nation until Pharaoh accepts that the God of Moses is not to be denied. We do not know by what name the Egyptians may later have spoken of the Hebrew deity. "The God of horror" or "the God of death" come to mind. But to the nation Moses leads through the Red Sea and away from oppression, the divine will be known hereafter as "the God who saves." Rescued from Egypt, the descendents of Israel pledge to keep the memory of this extraordinary experience at the heart of their relationship with God for all time. One of the oldest fragments of the Hebrew Scriptures is the song of salvation first sung at the far side of the Red Sea while Moses' sister Miriam leads the nation in a dance of celebration (see Exodus 15). Told and retold in psalms and prophecies, the story of this victory defines the relationship between God and the chosen people and gives them hope through all the difficult times to come.

We might take time here to consider what difference it makes *what* we call God. For example, we often use the name *Creator*, which is accurate enough for believers. But is it sufficient? When we call God Creator, we acknowledge a great power capable of wonderful imagination and beauty. We may be deeply impressed by such a God; we may feel wonder or gratitude. Yet using the name Creator may inadvertently limit the relationship. For the Deists of the eighteenth century, for example, God the Creator implied a one-dimensional contact. The Deists stopped right there with the notion of a God who created the world and then stepped back "indifferent, paring his fingernails" for all eternity, as James Joyce famously described it. Such a Creator may be a talented and admirable being, but that doesn't necessarily make the deity a friend of ours.

Knowing God as the God of Abraham or Israel, however, tells us that God chooses intimacy with the likes of us. This may assure us that, at least historically, God has taken a particular interest in humanity and has even engaged in a few remarkable interventions on our behalf. But consider the difference between knowing God as the one who saved a nation vs. knowing God as the one who *saves*. If saving is something God does—if saving is not simply an item on God's resume but is an aspect of God's nature—then that's very good news for the human race, perennially in need of a little saving…or a lot. No wonder the name *Savior* sticks with God up to the present time.

We should keep in mind that the story on record in the Bible is the one told by people of faith. Scholars are quick to point out that there were no doubt other members of the Hebrew nation who made it to the other side of the Red Sea and shouted, to no one in particular, "Lucky break!" Not viewing the events through the eyes of faith, they did not interpret what happened as God-inspired. We too can interpret our experiences as "charged with the grandeur of God," as Jesuit poet Gerard Manley Hopkins wrote, or simply the end result of a random roll of cosmic dice. If we see world events in light of our dealings with God (the Just Judge or Merciful Father or Suffering Lord), those names also influence how we interpret the meaning of our own stories.

The God of the Law
Naming God is like trying to pinpoint a moving target. God is infinite, eternal, omnipresent, omniscient and omnipotent. Any way we talk about God, we are still talking about a presence quite more expansive and complex than our own. It quickly becomes clear that one name for God is never going to be enough.

So the nation in the desert on the far side of the Red Sea comes to know the God who saves as the one who also sends manna and quail for their hunger and produces water from a rock on demand. God is likewise their champion in battle, as in the war against Amalek. But nothing matches the revelation of God on Mt. Sinai (also known as Mt. Horeb in Deuteronomy).

Here, the people have their first *theophany*, or encounter with the manifestation of God. A dense cloud appears over the mountain, followed by thunder and lightning, smoke, and a trumpet blast. The earth quakes and the sound grows cacophonous until the people are terrified. They beg Moses to speak to God *for* them, to ask God not to continue a personal encounter with the whole nation. As a result, from then on Moses confronts God alone.

On the mountain, God presents Moses with the *Decalogue*, more familiarly known as the Ten Commandments (see Exodus 20 and also Deuteronomy 5). With this Law, God establishes a new covenant with the nation, a promise literally set in stone. A covenant of law may seem "unbloody," but included in the several hundred other rules in the fine print is circumcision, not to mention animal sacrifice. The covenant with Moses still qualifies as one sealed in blood. Most of the rest of Exodus and nearly all of Leviticus, Numbers and Deuteronomy deal with the fine print of the Law attributed to Moses.

We may feel tempted to skip the many chapters about laws regarding slaves, thieves, property damage, and religious customs. And the plan for building the Ark of the Covenant, where the tablets of the Decalogue and the very power of God were understood to reside, is hardly thrilling narrative. Does it matter how many cubits of acacia wood go into constructing something that no longer exists, except in Indiana Jones' fantasies? And what's a cubit anyway?

My recommendation is to read as much of this material as you can for the story that emerges between the lines. For example, why are there rules regarding slaves at all, for a people who just got freed from slavery in Egypt? (Obviously, it wasn't belief in the natural right of freedom that motivated their escape but simple self-interest.) Other questions will arise, such as: Is "an eye for an eye" justice really the will of a compassionate God? (One answer: It was a radical concession in a culture that formerly took a *life* for an eye.)

The more time we spend considering the Mosaic law, the greater appreciation we have for its moral development over prevailing customs of the time. But we also get a sense of the limitations of culture that each generation strains against. Israel in the desert still had a long way to go to reach what we moderns would call *just*. Moral development rarely takes giant steps in one generation. The covenant of the Law by no means led to the perfect society—much less to the kingdom of God as Jesus would much later describe it. Even the Church as we know it today is not synonymous with the fulfillment of God's reign, as the Church's own teaching makes clear. If we're looking for God's will perfectly realized, we can't look to Exodus, or the Church, or any people in any hour of history. Growth takes time. Instruction is needed all along the way to lead us forward, the way children learn to add and subtract long before they are introduced to calculus. The Law of Moses may seem like a disappointing moral contract in twenty-first century terms, but God's relationship with humanity took a huge step forward through these documents. Though it may seem quaint or inadequate now, at the time the Law of Moses was a benchmark of ethical principle!

Sometimes, in order to really advance, we just have to make a paradigm shift altogether. Forty years in the desert might be considered a mighty long time to go on "retreat," but it helped the nation surrender its old identity and incorporate a new one.

The Desert Journey

The story of Exodus is about journey on many levels. *Exodus* means "the road out." The nation had to get out of Egypt, obviously. But it also had to get beyond a lot of behaviors and attitudes and ways of thinking that were also death dealing. The people of Israel had to leave behind the identity of slavery, which ran generations deep. They had to stop acting like those who are owned and mastered by the will of others. Instead, they had to learn to master themselves, as God once urged Cain to do. They had to learn to be God's people, not Pharaoh's. It is not easy for people to accept freedom, as Moses would discover. His job did not end when he led the people across the sea. It would take another forty years, a whole generation, to purge the nation of its slave mentality. Everyone who came out of

Egypt, even Moses himself, must die before the people can enter the land of promise.

The story of the desert is a difficult one, full of violence, disloyalty, and human stupidity. The long years of wandering lead to purification, however, and so the desert itself becomes one of the great symbols of the Bible. When the Hebrew prophets, the later Christian church fathers, or Jesus himself want to hear what God is saying without distraction or compromise, they each seek to recreate the Exodus experience, retreating to the desert to hunger, pray and wait. Some, like Ezekiel, have visions of heaven; others, like Jesus, meet the devil there. But through the experience of the desert, seekers are purged of their assumptions and worldly attachments and come to embrace the will of God more perfectly.

The journey of Israel in the desert is the journey each of us must take, in one form or another, if we seek a covenant with "the God who saves." Sin enslaves us from the moment our lives begin, and we struggle against its power to enthrall us daily. If we want to live with God, we have to die to everything that would fasten us to a lie about who we are and the freedom that is ours. Exodus is *our* story and *our* journey. Although we eventually emerge from our desert, as Israel does, we never quite leave behind its lessons.

Questions for Reflection and Discussion

1. Recall a time when you were rescued—physically, emotionally, spiritually. What did that experience teach you about your need for salvation?

2. Make a list of the names of God you know or use personally in prayer. What does each name teach you about the nature of God and your relationship with the divine?

3. Compare "the God who saves" of Israel in the Exodus story to the Savior we know in Jesus. How are they alike? How are they different?

4. The God of Exodus is introduced as a God of law. How is the God you know a God of law, and what are God's laws?

Should these laws be kept separate from human laws, or should they be the same? Explain your answer.

5. Recount a "desert experience" in your life when you have had to die to something in order to live for something else. What did you lose in the desert, and what did you gain from it?

Prayer Activity

Plan a time of exodus for the purpose of leaving some old way or identity behind. You may want to go on a weekend retreat or simply take a vacation to a solitary place. Your exodus may include starting a relationship with a spiritual director, a prayer group, a counselor, or a twelve-step program. The desert may be hard to cross, but every step leads you along the road out.

Joshua, Judges, 1 Samuel, 2 Samuel, 1 Kings,
2 Kings, 1 Chronicles, 2 Chronicles

Who Will Lead?

Authority operates in many settings: family, school, work, government, church. But it doesn't always operate well. The word *authority* implies power, particularly the power to decide. In Genesis, God is shown to be the original authority, and when humans challenged divinity with disobedience, the chafe of our submission to authority was first experienced. Human history continues to trace our love-hate relationship with people or institutions that represent authority. On some level, we know we need "higher powers" of one sort or another, but we also find ourselves in conflict with those who wield power over us. Can't we just all be in charge?

The short answer to that question is no. While personal autonomy is a healthy thing, anarchy gets messy as long as we persist in living as social beings. Good leadership is the best we can hope for, and that occurs when authority is used wisely, justly and compassionately. Unfortunately, this kind of leadership doesn't happen often. The Books of Joshua, Judges, Samuel and Kings mostly explore what happens when authority is misused and leadership fails.

Before the death of Moses, Joshua is selected to lead the people into the promised land of Canaan. Joshua has the right stuff to be a military leader, and Canaan will not be had without a fight. So here's the dilemma up front: God gave Canaan to the people of Israel, but nobody told the Hittites, Amorites, Canaanites, Perizzites, Hivites and Jebusites who currently lived there. Should they be slaughtered outright? Can a treaty be made to share the land? How about intermarriage? Remember, this is 1200 B.C., when diplomacy normally occurs at the end of a sword. We cannot know what God's instructions to Joshua might have been or, for that matter, what actually happened; we only know how the story was told.

45

Keeping Church teaching about Scripture in mind, our task is to discern *which* truth God wants us to learn from these stories. I think most of us would agree that mass murder is probably not a divine solution to a human problem. Yet it was the solution that came most readily to Joshua. The winners, as we know, write the history. And if you win, that must be God's will too, right? In the same way, when you lose, it must be because you have broken God's very complex and elaborate law. Or so the people of Joshua's time interpreted the events of their times.

And so Canaan is taken, one town at a time, starting with prized Jericho. Reading the Book of Joshua, you might get the impression that hardly a Canaanite was left standing at the end of the war, except the Hivites of Gibeon who sued for peace (see Joshua 11). But in fact, other parts of the Hebrew Scriptures tell another version of the story: that some truces were made, intermarriage did occur, and Israelites and Canaanites alike found ways to accommodate their new neighbors. War stories are like fish stories; they expand with the telling. Each of the twelve tribes of Israel gets a portion of the land, and Joshua dies at a ripe old age for a soldier. So now who's in charge of Israel? The question of leadership gets very interesting at this point.

First There Were Priests

Back in the time of Moses, the first high priest over Israel was appointed: Moses' brother Aaron. Was this a case of nepotism? Definitely: Aaron was certainly no great shakes as a leader. If you recall, he was implicated in the Golden Calf incident, a notorious act of idolatry that led to death and destruction.

Still, Aaron was not only made high priest but the men of his tribe, the Levites (descendents of Levi, one of the twelve children of Jacob), were declared a holy priesthood for all time. Some may find fault with today's seminary system, but priesthood by DNA had its problems as well. The tribe of Levi was entitled to a portion of the temple tithe in perpetuity. But we are getting ahead of our story. In the desert, there was as yet no temple—only the Tent of the Presence of the Lord, which contained the Ark of the Covenant. Moses, Aaron, and their sons were the only folks permitted to enter that holy space.

After reading the litany of rituals with holy utensils described in the Pentateuch, you might begin to suspect that most of this stuff could not have been hauled around the desert for forty years. The time of Moses was roughly 1300 B.C., and the Pentateuch took its final form before 500 B.C. Presumably, the rituals and sacred objects named in these books were added during the intervening centuries. Some authorities question whether the Levitical priesthood itself isn't a later development placed anachronistically into the story of Moses. As we've noted before, much is included in the "books of Moses" for the purpose of sharing his mantel of authority.

The office of priesthood certainly wasn't invented for Aaron. According to the biblical record, Abraham and Jacob clearly fulfilled priestly functions as patriarchs of their families: building altars, offering sacrifices, dealing with God on behalf of their people. Foreign priests, like Melchizedek of Salem and Jethro of Midian, make their appearances before Aaron ever took office. Although priests are never officially in charge of the nation, they do exercise a certain amount of leadership. Before the Jerusalem Temple comes into being, priests keep shrines dedicated to the Lord on the high places and are sought out for the negotiating of sacrificial offerings there. But the track record of priestly leadership throughout the biblical accounts is spotty. Eli and his sons fail in their commission at Shiloh with disastrous results (see 1 Samuel 2). Abiathar becomes a "priest of David" along with Zadok at the original Temple in Jerusalem, but he backs the wrong heir in the succession wars after David's reign (see 1 Kings 2). In the Books of Maccabees, the question of legitimate priesthood arises when the heir to Zadok is ousted. It is a rare priest like Zechariah, the father of John the Baptist, who seems a decent sort, raising his little son with an aging wife long after most couples put such work aside (see Luke 1).

But notoriety wins out: The priests we remember best are Annas and Caiaphas, leaders of the Sanhedrin at the time of Jesus. Caiaphas, who utters the fateful words, "It is better for you to have one man die for the people than to have the whole nation destroyed" (John 11:50), reflects in this statement the role of the priest as presider over the sacrifice. He and Annas will also bring charges against Peter and John in the early church (see Acts 4). It is no wonder that Jesus will be identified as a new kind of High Priest in the Letter to the Hebrews, one who *is* the sacrifice that he offers. Jesus receives the title of High Priest "according to the order of Melchizedek," however—not the order of Aaron. Melchizedek, a Canaanite ally of Abraham, was both priest and king of ancient Salem, later Jerusalem (see Genesis 14). Melchizedek's priesthood predated the Levites and thus sidesteps the question of their authority.

This brief survey of the biblical priesthood may suggest why the nation looked to some other form of leadership for its governance.

Then There Were Judges

So what about the judges? This office also dates to the time of Moses, when his father-in-law Jethro (himself a Midianite priest) notices that his son-in-law is besieged by appeals for decisions night and day. "What you are doing is not good," Jethro informs him. "You will surely wear yourself out, both you and these people with you" (Exodus 18:17–18). He counsels Moses to appoint elders to judge over the people, and the position endures for generations.

Judges are a terrific innovation that make Moses' life easier. They also contribute some of the most colorful characters to the canon of Scripture. Without judges we would not have mighty Samson (and Delilah); Deborah the wise, also a prophetess and leader of armies; Gideon and his divining fleece; Ehud the left-handed, who slays a king so obese that the hilt of his sword disappears into the king's belly; or dark Jephthah, who makes a terrible oath for which his young daughter pays with her life. Samuel the prophet and priest is likewise called a judge, although he is not among the twelve whose deeds are recounted in the Book of Judges. We can see from this short list that ancient offices of leadership were not mutually exclusive or neatly defined.

Truthfully, most of the judges in Judges are portrayed as military leaders rather than wisdom figures, except for Deborah who is both. Judges wield their authority through divine

48

decree—sort of. Which is to say that God was always behind the chosen judges, but not all the judges got behind the Lord in the same way. For example, Samson's miraculous strength depends on his keeping the Nazarite oath not to cut his hair. We know how that works out. We also see that Gideon's strength is not in physique nor surely in numbers, as he leads an army of three hundred to victory over three nations. Is his strength, then, from God? Yes. Is Gideon ready to serve the will of God? Not by a long shot. Read Judges 6–7 for a good chuckle at how Gideon wins the war despite himself.

Deborah, by contrast, has the kind of mettle needed to lead her constituency in wisdom, war, and the ways of God. She is perhaps the only major judge shown to be a worthy authority figure. Her greatest military victory is attained in cooperation with the efforts of another woman, Jael. When the song of this conquest is later sung, even the mother of the vanquished general plays a role in it. The story of salvation, rarely told in terms of its women, takes its feminine side out for a spin here, as happens elsewhere in the historical books of Israel. (See the chapter on "Woman in Salvation History" for more on Deborah.)

Jephthah, however, reveals the shadow side of the judge's authority. He makes a vow to God that in return for a victory over the Ammonites he will make a human sacrifice of whoever greets him first upon his return. We hear the discordant note at once. Didn't he learn from the story of Abraham and Isaac that Israelites are forbidden to make human holocaust to God? And since when does God accept bribes from the divinely appointed leader? Nonetheless, Jephthah does win the battle, only to be greeted upon his return by his own daughter, who comes out to him trustingly with music and dancing. Jephthah is too proud to retreat from his oath, and his only child is too pious and obedient not to submit to it. She asks for time to mourn her virginity with her friends in the mountains before she is sacrificed. Many who read this story in Judges 11 lament that no angel arrived to stop the sacrifice, as in the story of Isaac. Jepthah's proud oath remains in bitter contrast to Abraham's honest struggle with traditional pagan practice. The office of the judges, fraught with human error like the priesthood, does not survive beyond the time of Samuel.

Prophets and Kings

In every age, prophets and kings need each other. Kings control the seats of power and represent conservatism, commerce and stability. Prophets, on the other hand, are the wild cards of authority. They scurry around on the edge of things with their challenging and destabilizing critique. They argue and accuse, and ultimately those at the center of power either relent to the prophet or kill him or her. This is true not only in the Bible but in every generation. Contrast Catherine of Siena with the pope in Avignon; Martin Luther King, Jr. with government opponents of civil rights; Oscar Romero with the ruling class of El Salvador; Cesar Chavez and Dolores Huerta with the farm owners. Prophets and kings are in a symbiotic relationship that is both inevitable and volatile. You could say that kings *cause* prophets—not that they ever intend to.

But it wasn't always this way. In the Hebrew story, prophets predate kings. It is hard to say who the first biblical prophet is, since the voice of prophecy is heard whenever anyone presumes to speak for God. In this sense, Abraham and Moses are prophets. But the first full-time appointed prophet seems to be Samuel. His mother Hannah jumpstarts his career by vowing before God to sacrifice her son, spiritually speaking, to the service of the Lord before Samuel is even conceived. After weaning him, Hannah hands over her son to Eli the priest of Shiloh to be raised as a Nazarite.

Eli and his sons are unfaithful priests, but that doesn't keep Eli from recognizing the voice of God when the Lord first speaks to Samuel. Eli teaches Samuel the correct reply: "Speak, Lord, for your servant is listening"(1 Samuel 3:9). In this way, the boy learns the essence of his trade as a prophet.

Samuel's sons, however, are not like their father, choosing the crooked route to success by accepting bribes for their judgments. Appointed to succeed Samuel as judges, they are rejected by the elders of Israel who demand, instead, a king to rule over them so that Israel can take its place among the nations. Samuel, however, sees error in this direction. Until now, Israel has been a *theocracy*—that is, a God-ruled nation with priests, judges and prophets mediating the relationship. This new political direction would indeed lead Israel to take its place among the nations as greedy, militant, power-mongering and idolatrous. When Samuel spells out for the people the disastrous nature of monarchies, they remain adamant. Samuel reluctantly delivers their request to the Lord, and God assures him the people will get precisely what they are asking for.

The kingship of Saul is the result. Anointed to rule, Saul is impatient, belligerent, insecure and, worst of all, disobedient in relationship to the Lord. Samuel tries to serve and warn his king, but in the end Saul suffers a profound depression that has a touch of madness in it. Samuel slips off to Bethlehem to anoint Saul's successor, the young and unlikely David. The relationship between prophets and kings is cemented in this subversive and inflammatory act. Future kings will have their puppet-like court prophets, while the genuine item remains the free-lance operator who speaks only for God.

The Covenant with David

Why do some leaders succeed where others fail? Saul's reign soured almost at once, whereas David is a hero when he first steps up to battle Goliath. From his youth, David was neither strong nor charismatic like Saul, yet his quiet trust in God becomes a far greater power to contend with. David forms a close friendship with Saul's son and heir, Jonathan, a friendship that seals both their fates: David is destined to rise, and Jonathan is to fall along with his father.

Like every biblical hero before him, David is a wonderfully flawed and complicated character. He takes several wives—Michal, the daughter of Saul, as well as Abigail and Ahinoam—not to mention someone else's wife, Bathsheba. Nor is he above intrigue and murder, as his treatment of his faithful general Uriah (unfortunate husband of Bathsheba) makes clear. David sees the Law as subordinate to practical concerns, allowing his soldiers to eat the holy bread from the Temple (a move Jesus later salutes when he is accused of breaking the Sabbath). David is not restrained by the dignity of office as he dances half-naked before the Ark of the Covenant in the sight of his people. Although God betrays no interest in establishing a temple, David insists on building one.

David also shows tremendous resolve. Even as Saul plots to destroy him, David refuses to kill his king, though he has his opportunities. David repents his adultery with Bathsheba as soon as the prophet Nathan accuses him of it, accepting the death of their son as the price of his deed. And perhaps because he struggles so hard to be faithful—to his God, his king, his friend Jonathan, his wives, Bathsheba, and all the children to emerge from his tangled unions—David is the recipient of God's next covenant. David and his house are established to rule forever. That's a long time in human terms. And yet David's kingdom, or at least its earthly dimension, is shattered within one generation.

The effects of sin continue to trump David's best intentions. His wives and children are a jumble of loyalties that cannot be held together in one place. Pretty soon the fighting starts, and these dark hours include rape, incest, fratricide, and an attempt at patricide/regicide. David manages to survive it all and hands over the kingdom to Solomon, second son of Bathsheba, before his death. Ironically, David's complex and troubled rule is also Israel's finest hour. The monarchy goes downhill from here. Solomon's kingdom does increase in wealth, and under his rule the Temple is finally completed. But the man called the wisest who ever lived couldn't avoid his father's mistakes: the multiplicity of wives and the fragmentation of loyalty. By comparison, Solomon makes David look like a celibate—and the kingdom of Israel does not recover from his excesses.

Priests, judges, prophets, kings. That's a whole lot of leadership, but the question of who's in charge and where ultimate authority resides has yet to be answered.

Questions for Reflection and Discussion

1. Describe your relationship to authority in family, education, work, government, church. What might have to

change in order to heal your relationship to authority in each of these areas?

2. What kind of authority should religious leaders have, and how far should it extend? Is the separation between church and state possible? Why or why not?

3. Who might serve as the "judges" in our present system: legal experts, military leaders, political representatives, economic advisors, scholars, church authorities or others? What are the advantages and drawbacks of following each group's lead?

4. Identify some contemporary "prophets" and "kings" who are locked in a relationship of power and challenge. Where do today's prophets come from?

5. What was King David's greatest asset? What was his biggest mistake? How does the covenant with David parallel previous covenants, and what makes it unique?

Prayer Activity

Reflect on those who represent authority in your life: your parents living or deceased, mentors, bosses, spouses, children, church, government, media, or other sources that influence you in powerful ways. Consider ways your relationship to authority may be out of balance and need adjustment. What would change if God was truly the ultimate authority in your life?

1 Kings, 2 Kings
Isaiah, Ezekiel, Jeremiah
Hosea, Joel, Amos, Obadiah, Jonah, Micah, Nahum,
Habbakkuk, Zephaniah, Haggai, Zechariah, Malachi

Who Will Follow?

Leaders may lead—but who will follow? In the animal kingdom, genetic imprinting makes it easy: baby ducks follow mother ducks, and ants follow the chemical trail laid down by the scout. For human beings, it's a little more complicated: Someone may blaze a trail, but no one may follow. For this reason, presidents lose their mandate, pastors are moved, and school boards revolve. Just as prophets and kings are inextricably linked, so are leaders and followers. Successful leaders attract others to journey together toward a common goal.

Unfortunately, many leaders acquire power for personal benefit and disdain their supporters, making enemies instead of alliances. So goes human history with its wars and rumors of wars. Humanity history is far from finished with the clash of might, wealth and prerogative.

The story of Israel's kings demonstrates how often power blinds leaders to their purpose, which is to serve by an appropriate use of authority. The Books of Kings and Chronicles review a litany of devastating decisions made by rulers. Solomon, for example, builds the Temple and thereby crushes the nation with taxes. (Note that it takes him seven years to build the Temple–and thirteen years to build his own palace.) God granted Solomon wisdom, but wisdom does not guarantee the will to do right. The Temple in which Solomon prides himself will become a heap of ruins if king and people are not faithful to their God.

A man with seven hundred wives and three hundred concubines probably has trouble being single-hearted. His foreign wives expect shrines raised to their own gods, which threatens Israel's allegiance to the one God. Although Solomon rules until his death, the seeds of division are planted in his reign. The nation is split into two kingdoms, Israel to the north and Judah to the south. Solomon's son inherits Judah with its capital in Jerusalem and its Temple. But what no one inherits is the idea that the leader must also follow a higher authority. More than forty kings will rule the south and the north, yet few follow the God of the covenant. Meanwhile, God, faithful even when we are false, sends prophets "early and often" to remind the nation who is out in front of them.

The Early Prophets

Nobody likes a prophet. Consider a time you may have been called upon to speak the truth when others had decided to bow before a lie. Whether such moments occur on the playground, at the office, or within your own family, they can be painful and fearful. People committed to a convenient or profitable lie are hardened against hearing the truth. So if you tell an unpopular truth, prepare to be dismissed, hounded or humiliated. Rarely does anyone say to a prophet, "Oh, thank you, you're absolutely right!"

Prophecy is even more dangerous when the truth threatens the agenda of those in power. When power is maintained at the expense of truth, speaking truthfully creates risk and vulnerability on both sides—which is why writers may be jailed, theologians silenced, and prophets in every land routinely killed. When truth is "the enemy," powerful people will find ways to suppress it, though ultimately they cannot keep it from being declared. Jesus spoke often about the invincibility of the truth. When the crowds of Jerusalem sang his praises, the Pharisees ordered Jesus to quiet the masses, fearing a riot. Jesus replied, "I tell you, if they keep silent, the stones will cry out!" (Luke 19:40) God's creation, animated with truth, would be hard to overcome. Sooner or later, what is whispered in the dark will be spoken in the light (see Matthew 10:26–27).

In the time of King Ahab and perhaps for all time, never was there a prophet like Elijah for speaking truth to power. Elijah was such a luminous figure that the Jewish community still sets a place for him each year at the Passover meal. Jewish tradition has it that Elijah's return will precipitate the coming of the *Messiah*, the anointed one of God who will save his people and rule with divine authority. John the Baptist was often confused with Elijah because he spoke with a prophet's passion and directed the crowds to Jesus.

What gives Elijah such prestige among the biblical prophets? He successfully predicts a drought in Israel—which he survives out in the desert by being fed by ravens. He rewards a widow's kindness with an unending supply of oil and flour. He fights "fire with fire" against the prophets of Baal and wins, to the humiliation of Ahab's queen Jezebel. Eventually, both king and queen want nothing more than to see Elijah dead. Due to their relentless persecution, the day arrives when Elijah agrees with them and prays for his own death. Instead, God sends an angel to revive him for the journey ahead. That journey leads to Elisha, who becomes Elijah's attendant and successor—but not upon his death, for Elijah never dies. He is one of a tiny minority of biblical people who simply return to God mysteriously. For example, Enoch "walks with God" in Genesis and is seen no more, and according to tradition Mary, the mother of Jesus, is assumed bodily into heaven at the end of her earthly life. Elijah, with his usual dramatic flair, is carried into the heavens by a fiery chariot until he is lost from view. To the end, the prophet remains a tough act to follow.

But Elisha does follow that act—and with a double portion of his master's spirit. He performs literally twice as many miracles as Elijah. Elisha "heals" bad water and makes it drinkable, restores a poisoned stew, feeds a hundred men with multiplied bread, and heals a foreign general of leprosy. He goes so far as to bring a dead child back to life, while causing the deaths of other children who taunt him. He presides over the grisly death of Jezebel and anoints a new king over the northern kingdom. A few kings later, Elisha finally dies, but a dead man accidentally tossed into his grave is restored to life by contact with Elisha's bones. Even in death, Elisha reveals the power of God.

The Time of the Writing Prophets

Sherlock Holmes had Dr. Watson to record his achievements,

and Samuel Johnson had his Boswell to commit his conversation to print. But neither Elijah nor Elisha had a biographer, though they may have been the greatest of the biblical prophets. No one wrote down their best speeches or kept a log of their quotable quotes. That's why, when we speak of prophets, we often think first of the fellows who have books named after them, otherwise known as the *writing* prophets. The writing prophets controlled their legacy by setting it down personally—more or less, though certainly some of what appears under a prophet's name may have been written by later adherents to his school of thought.

But before we look at individual writing prophets, we should ask certain questions about the context in which they lived and wrote. First, who is their audience: northern Israel or southern Judah? The northern kingdom is destined to disappear from the story (hence the legend of the ten "lost" tribes), and Judah to the south will become the *de facto* Israel ever after. From a historical perspective, the prophets to the north were engaged in a lost cause. Second, at what time in history is the prophet writing: before, during, or after 587 B.C.? It's a date to keep in mind, for that's the year when Jerusalem is conquered and the nation goes into exile in Babylon. Each writing prophet is therefore positioned as a voice of warning, hope or celebration in relation to the exile. (To assist in pinpointing the prophets within history, see their time line in the appendices.) Third, what are the prophet's issues: religious infidelity, political corruption, economic injustice—or all three? Prophets address the agenda embedded in their age, and recognizing this helps us to appreciate their words. When we hear the prophets read in church, we often have no context in which to hear their message. Timelessness is one characteristic of genuine prophecy, and so it is appropriate for us to relate ancient prophecies to our generation and its issues. But to fully and accurately trace the parallels between a prophet's age and ours, it helps to know the situation he or she was originally addressing.

By this time it must be clear that biblical prophecy rarely means fortune-telling about the future, which is our popular sense of the word. Biblical prophets are much more concerned with the *present*. Their message, frequently in the form of an *oracle* or "word of the Lord," is aimed squarely at their own time and circumstance. They may predict an upcoming scenario, but more often they present alternative futures based on decisions to be made in the present: If you persist in doing A, B will befall you; however, if you do C, God will relent and do D. In other words, prophets don't foretell the future so much as emphasize the people's responsibility to choose a future thoughtfully. They remind their audience, then and now, that we are made in the image of our creator God and it is up to us to co-create our world wisely.

The Major Prophets

Three of the writing prophets are known as the *major prophets*: Isaiah, Jeremiah and Ezekiel. They are major not necessarily because they are more important but because their legacies are more substantial. That is, each has an entire scroll dedicated to his work. But there the similarity ends. Each major prophet has a unique style and flavor: Isaiah is a remarkable poet, Jeremiah is profoundly personal, Ezekiel is a bit of a visionary madman. Taken together, these three reveal much about the God they passionately represent.

Of the three, Isaiah appears first on the scene—as well as second and third! Most scholars believe the book we call "Isaiah" had authors in three generations. The historical Isaiah writes chapters 1 through 39 around 742 B.C. in the southern kingdom of Judah, well before the Exile. Deutero-Isaiah (chapters 40 through 55) writes to the people in Babylon, where the issues have changed. Trito-Isaiah (chapters 56 through 66) takes up the prophetic call again after the people are restored to their land. This collection of writings over hundreds of years demonstrates the enduring influence of the prophet and his message.

Isaiah is probably the most quotable prophet, and composers from Handel through contemporary hymnists have appreciated his lyricism. Without the school of Isaiah, think of what would be missing from Advent: "The people who walked in darkness have seen a great light" (9:2); from Christmas: "For a child has been born for us, a son given to us" (9:6); from Lent:

"In the wilderness prepare the way of the Lord!" (40:3); from Good Friday: "I did not hide my face from insult and spitting" (50:6); from Easter Vigil: "Everyone who thirsts, come to the waters!" (55:1); from penance: "Wash yourselves; make yourselves clean" (1:16); from the peace movement: "They shall beat their swords into plowshares" (2:4); from consolation: "Comfort, O comfort my people" (40:1). Theologians suggest that Jesus came to his radical understanding of the role of Israel's awaited Messiah by reading the suffering servant songs of Isaiah.

The prophet Jeremiah (c. 621–587 B.C.) is a whole new ballgame. If Isaiah described the role of the suffering servant, Jeremiah *lived* it. He was the prophet most likely to be assassinated—and according to tradition, he was. Meanwhile he got arrested, beaten, imprisoned, thrown into a muddy cistern, and endured a lifetime of rejection and public disgrace. If that weren't bad enough, Jeremiah was the first practicing celibate on the Hebrew record. Against all cultural norms, he refrained from marriage and begetting as a sign that the nation's future was imperiled (see 16:2).

The prophet as signpost was Jeremiah's specialty. Elijah and Elisha were known for miraculous action and later prophets for their bold words. Yet symbolic action was also part of the prophet's duty. Isaiah went naked for three years to underscore the vulnerability of the nation (see 20:3). Jeremiah took up the practice of being a "word made flesh," wearing a yoke around his neck and tramping through Jerusalem predicting servitude (see 27:2) and smashing a potter's flask to illustrate the fate of the city (see 19:10). He also refuses to share in events of either mourning or celebration, demonstrating how far the people have removed themselves from God's consolation and joy (see 16:5–9). Jeremiah's life is united with his words in a way so personal that today we know him better than any other figure in the Hebrew Scriptures. Jeremiah bares for us the soul of the prophet in its anguish and indecision. He has been called a prototype of Jesus, and in the end he too was murdered at the hands of his countrymen.

Ezekiel's prophetic contribution is made during the exile in

Babylon. He is the first prophet to receive his call outside of the Holy Land, and his message reflects this distinction. Unlike Isaiah and Jeremiah who were up to their necks in politics, Ezekiel's fascination lay with the Temple and liturgy—both dear in his recollections of Israel, since he (like Jeremiah) was a priest. Ezekiel is considered the father of modern Judaism, for it was his task to develop a way of being faithful to God apart from the service of the earthly Temple.

If Isaiah is known chiefly for his poetry and Jeremiah for his signs, Ezekiel is memorable for his visions, vast and mysterious. *Chariots of the Gods,* the book and movie speculating on traces of alien contact with earth, employed Ezekiel's colorful descriptions, although Ezekiel's God was more Jewish than true believers in the movie might allow. The first twenty chapters of his prophecy contain little narrative, driven by a tête-à-tête the prophet has with God, although these oracles were aimed at specific audiences to whom they were likely delivered later. The prophet is lifted up and brought to Jerusalem in "visions" in which he witnesses God's glory departing from the city (see chapters 8-10). The most familiar passage is the vision of the dry bones (see chapter 37), as the prophet watches God reassemble the broken nation. As the song goes, even "dem dry bones" won't stay dead if God chooses to restore them to life.

The Minor Prophets

A word of advice to hopeful evangelists: If you want to be remembered, don't collaborate. In the case of the Old Testament, collaboration includes writing so little that your words are dumped into the common grave of a communal scroll. The twelve *minor prophets*—Hosea, Joel, Amos, Obadiah, Micah, Nahum, Habakkuk, Zephaniah, Haggai, Zechariah, Malachi and Jonah—share this dismissive fate, and our brief survey here will prove no exception. Not that the minor prophets aren't interesting in their own right! I'd put Jonah up against any other short narrative in the Bible for sheer story value, and each of these books lends an insightful peek into the ongoing understanding of who God is and what God wants.

But they get short shrift in the lectionary and so remain

61

obscure to us. Amos and Hosea are the first prophets to put stylus to parchment, writing around the mid-700s B.C. to Israel in the north, the territory of the early prophets. Hosea condemns religious infidelity through an allegory about his marriage to an unfaithful woman, Gomer, who may or may not have been historical. Amos is remarkable for three reasons. One, he is a shepherd from the *south* who feels compelled to prophesy to the *north*. Two, he brings an angry message with little hope—a departure from the usual premise that God is merciful in the face of repentance. And finally, Amos' dark mood inspires a parody, the Book of Jonah (between the fifth and third centuries B.C.), about a fictitious prophet who prefers to see a sinful city destroyed rather than converted. The writer of Jonah transforms Amos's ending: God does show mercy as the city repents, and Jonah must repent as well and accept God's choice to be compassionate.

The last of four eighth-century prophets, Micah (750 B.C.) is memorable to Christians for his expectation that hope will one day come from the town of Bethlehem. Zephaniah, Nahum and Habakkuk all prophesy in the late seventh century B.C. Zephaniah has a significant influence on Jeremiah's prophecy that follows it. Nahum rails against Nineveh, the Assyrian city prophets love to hate (see Jonah.) Of course, when Nineveh finally does fall, it means that Jerusalem will soon follow. (One should not claim "God's will" too heartily regarding the bad fortune of one's enemies.) Habakkuk takes the interesting route of calling God to task for the mess the world is in—possibly the first prophet to do so but hardly the last.

After the exile, Haggai speaks first (520 B.C.). Not surprisingly, his concern is the Temple, which must be rebuilt upon Israel's return to their homeland. His contemporary, Zechariah, is also concerned with religious matters, although remembered by Christians mostly for contributing two Holy Week images: the king who rides into Jerusalem on an ass (see 9:9) and "the one whom they have pierced" (12:10). Obadiah, Joel and Malachi follow, but their dates are obscure. Obadiah is distinguished for being the shortest book in the Old Testament. (It escapes being the shortest in the Bible because of the brief letters of John.) Joel focuses on the ominous Day of the Lord, which we hear about each year on Ash Wednesday. Malachi, ranting against corrupt priests, is the last voice heard in the Hebrew Scriptures. Because his prophecy ends with the word "doom"—a bad note on which to end your holy books— ancient writers repeated at the end of the scroll his next-to-the-last verse, a saying that looks forward to Elijah's return.

The prophetic worldview is so radically different from the Pentateuch and historical books that we may wonder how both traditions emerged in roughly the same time period. Presumably the centers of power commissioned the first set of writings, while the prophetic tradition arose from the margins. Even today, both traditions remain in tension, as leaders and prophets vie for control of "the vision thing."

Questions for Reflection and Discussion

1 Give an example of tension between leaders and followers in our society. How must leaders also "follow" if they are to successfully lead?

2. What do you think the world need more of today: miraculous deeds, compelling words, or people who are "living signs"? Defend your answer.

3. Which of the three major prophets seems especially relevant today? Cite one passage of prophecy that sounds appropriate to contemporary times, and explain why.

4. Read one of the minor writing prophets who is less familiar to you. Do you think his message is still meaningful in our society? Explain.

5. When have you been called upon to speak the truth prophetically in situations you have faced? Who has spoken prophetically to you in your life?

Prayer Activity

Consider ways your life is or can become a living sign of God's presence and concern in the world. Identify a contemporary prophet and read more about his or her message for our times.

Ruth, Judith, Esther, Judges, Joshua,
1 Samuel, Genesis

The Women of Salvation History

Some may wonder why a chapter about women is included in a book about the Hebrew Scriptures. Aren't all the main actors in the Old Testament men? After all, we don't call them the patriarchs for nothing!

Others may feel that shuttling women's stories to a separate chapter marginalizes them all over again. Shouldn't women take their place among the big boys of salvation history?

My hope is to honor these women by giving them a spotlight here. In a book this small about a tradition so enormous, it is hard to do justice to every person and theme, and some of your favorites, like mine, are going to end up on the cutting room floor. In the story of salvation, it can seem as though that has already happened to the women.

The first editor of any story is its author, and the authors of the Bible were predominantly if not exclusively men. Male authors were predisposed to tell a story in terms of the exploits of men. Given that reality, an astonishing number of women are represented in the tradition. Nearly two hundred women appear *by name* in the Bible, with an additional hundred identified only in relationship to men, such as Potiphar's wife or Jephthah's daughter. Finally, several dozen more are known simply for what they did, like "the woman accused of adultery" or "the woman who raised her voice in the crowd."

With more than three hundred women featured in the Bible, it's challenging to see how many we can list. Somewhere between Eve of Eden and Mary of Nazareth, we've nurtured a vast ignorance about the women on the business end of all that begetting. Part of the problem is traditional religious education.

65

Salvation history is generally taught by connecting the dots from Noah to Abraham to Moses and on through kings, prophets and apostles, as if God only made divine deals with men. Culturally, we're still biased in this direction, and female religion teachers will lean toward this approach as unconsciously as their male counterparts.

But we can't lay the fault simply at the door of the nun or the CCD teacher who first told us the story. For most Catholics, the readings we hear at Mass are our main pipeline to the tradition. The lectionary is a highly selective book that presents salvation history geared toward the seasons of the church year. This means some stories will be heard a lot and some are never told at all. Is this why the books with women's names—Ruth, Judith and Esther—are read *very rarely* at Mass and *never* on a Sunday?

It's hard to deny that women in salvation history have been sidelined, first by the writers of Scripture, second by the writers and teachers of religious education, and third in the context of our liturgy. So how do we reclaim them in our heritage? Where should we begin?

Villainesses and Victims

Behind every man in the Bible there's a woman—and sometimes a handful or a harem-full. Like their male counterparts, not all women in the Bible are nice, and even the heroines are as flawed as Bible heroes tend to be. Scripture writers didn't intend to present sterling examples of how we ought to live as God's people. They recount the choices God's people have made so far and invite us into the biblical story. So when we go hunting for biblical women, we can expect they will be no better and no worse than biblical men.

If we brainstorm for the women of Scripture, the usual result is something like this: Eve, Sarah, Delilah, Jezebel, Mary Magdalene and Mary of Nazareth. What a lineup! Chances are, this list owes more to art and the movies than anything else. These women pose for more cameos than other biblical women because they are larger than life. Big sinners and big saints tend to get all the limelight.

When you really wrack your brain for the biblical women you've heard about in church or school, you may notice that the names start falling into two columns: villainesses and victims. The villainesses may be easiest to come up with. Some of them are objectively evil, like Jezebel, King Ahab's wife. She wants to see the prophets die in order to enjoy her queenly comforts guilt-free. When the dogs lick her blood from the pavements in the end, no one sheds a tear (see 2 Kings 10). Or take Potiphar's wife, who throws herself at young Joseph and then cries rape when he remains unresponsive (see Genesis 39). Delilah, Samson's seducer and self-appointed hairdresser, is likewise pitiless. She is one of a number of women who use sexuality to tempt a great man to fall (see Judges 16). The jury is still out on whether Bathsheba is more villain or victim: Did she flaunt her beauty to catch David's eye, or was she taken by the king against her will and widowed in the process? (See 2 Samuel 11.)

Susanna, spied upon by lascivious old men and then handed over for stoning when she will not submit to them (see the addition to the Book of Daniel), is an example of the victim female, the "damsel in distress" familiar in every aspect of literature from Greek mythology to last night's cop show. Dinah, Jacob's only daughter, is a classic victim character, first raped by Shechem and then further shamed by her brothers' murderous response (see Genesis 34). David's daughter Tamar is victimized by her half-brother and then suffers his scorn when his passion turns to hatred (see 2 Samuel 13). These stories are unhappily legion in antiquity, and they only get worse. Lot is willing to offer his two virgin daughters to appease a lustful crowd in Sodom that is bent on raping his houseguest (see Genesis 19). In another story of ancient Israel, the body of an abused and murdered concubine is cut up into pieces, which are then distributed around the towns to advertise the injustice (see Judges 19). As horrendous as these stories are, similar outrages appear in our newspapers to this day.

Other women in Scripture straddle the moral fence between villainess and victim. Who is more vilified than Eve, most often presented as the mother of original sin? Yet Eve is also a victim of primordial ignorance and a wily serpent, and as the mother of all the living deserving of some respect (see Genesis 1-3). Sarah, Abraham's wife, occupies the fence as well. By lying about their relationship—"She is my sister"—her husband trades her off a time or two in exchange for free passage through foreign lands. This bad treatment is coupled with years of pressure to produce a nation of heirs, which Sarah finally attempts to do by offering her servant girl, Hagar, to Abraham. It is impossible to know if Hagar found this a detestable or privileged situation, but in any case it ended badly for both women, as Sarah feels upstaged and Hagar is beaten by her mistress and compelled to run away. Is Hagar the only victim here? And do not both women, in their own way, show something more than mere longsuffering in their characters? (See Genesis 16.)

The lines are similarly blurred in the case of Rebekah, Isaac's wife, who favors one son over the other and sets in motion the events leading to Jacob's ascendancy over Esau. Does she do God's will, diverting the stream of salvation history to the one who will become the namesake of Israel? Or is she an interfering mother and dishonest wife? (See Genesis 27.)

And what about Rachel, second wife of Jacob and first in his heart? Her scourge was that her sister Leah was given to her husband on the night that should have been her wedding night (see Genesis 29). She is remembered also as the mother of lamentation: "Rachel is weeping for her children; she refuses to be comforted for her children, because they are no more" (Jeremiah 31:15). One may designate her a victim of salvation history, but then we recall how she stole her father's idols and kept the knowledge from her husband, jeopardizing the entire camp in the process. We might argue that Laban and Jacob had it coming to them, but would it ever be the will of Israel's God for someone to lie, cheat and steal, especially when it involves *idols*? These are morally muddy waters for sure (see Genesis 31).

Miracle Moms

There is a third category of biblical women that has no complement in the stories of men: the miracle moms. Here we find those rare women who would not have been mothers at all if not for the direct intervention of God's will. The New Testament figures of Mary of Nazareth and her cousin Elizabeth immediately spring to mind in this category. Their prototypes in the Hebrew Scriptures are Sarah, Hannah, and the Shunammite woman in 2 Kings 4. Because they belong to such an exclusive club, it is useful to look at these five women together, even though two are technically beyond the scope of this book. All five reveal the literary elements of the miracle birth story and how we are to understand it.

Miracle moms are stock characters in ancient literature. They are significant, not necessarily because of who they are in themselves but because of the sons (invariably) they are destined to bear. Miracle moms are mostly spotless people: Mary, Elizabeth, Hannah and Mrs. Shunammite are all fairly perfect (although Mary alone has doctrine to back it up). Sarah breaks the mold, being a morally checkered character as we have already noted.

Miracle moms routinely have the birth foretold to them by God's representative: an angel, a priest, or a prophet in these five cases. Other features of this type of story show more variations. For example, all miracle moms respond to the announcement of the birth in *some* way, but not in the *same* way. Two of the five biblical mothers sing about the news, although which two is unclear: Hannah certainly does, and someone during Mary's visitation with Elizabeth produces a similar canticle, although it is ambiguous who the singer is. (Mary gets credit for it in the popular tradition, but scholars are less sure.) Sarah only laughs at the news; the Shunammite woman actively protests.

The exact nature of the miracle that makes them miracle moms also varies from story to story. Sarah and Elizabeth have never had children and are now far too old. They have been deemed barren in an age when childlessness was considered strictly a female disorder. In the Shunammite story, however, we are told that her *husband* is getting on in years. Hannah is younger and more objectively "barren," since her husband's other wife has borne several children while Hannah remains childless. Mary alone becomes a mother without the intervention of a man. All five women attribute the miracle to God.

69

How these women got involved in miraculous goings-on is the most individual aspect of the matter. God's representatives deal directly with the husbands of Sarah and Elizabeth in revealing the plan; neither woman is consulted nor her cooperation sought. Do these elderly women want to be the mothers of infants? No one asks. In the Shunammite story, Elisha solicits advice about what might be done to repay the woman's kindness and is told by others that she laments having no son. Hannah alone is proactive in the situation. She begs God for a child. So fervent is her prayer at the shrine that the priest concludes she must be drunk. Hannah offers God a deal: She'll consecrate the child to God's purposes as soon as it is weaned, if she might just conceive. It's a peculiar bid, but successful. Not only does Hannah give birth to the prophet Samuel, but after she surrenders him God grants her five more children. She is the only miracle mom who is recorded as having more than one child.

Mary of Nazareth, of course, holds a privileged place among miraculous mothers. Her virginity is not the only reason for that, nor is the unique identity of her son. In strictly human terms, she is the only woman God addresses proactively in making the divine deal. (At least, that's Luke's account. Matthew reverts to the more familiar pattern, establishing Joseph as the main actor and bartering the deal between God and him.)

Although other categories of biblical women may still be open for new candidates in present and future generations, chances are we won't see many more miracle moms. (Unless we count our own, of course, which is a point we need not debate.)

Other Women to Consider

Regrettably, pop culture has favored the stories of biblical villainesses and victims. Mentally review the Sunday afternoons you've spent watching movies about the delicious villainy of Jezebel (as interpreted by Paulette Goddard), Delilah (Elizabeth Hurley), or Bathsheba (Susan Hayward). Because their stories get more airtime, these are the biblical women most folks recognize and can name. Religious educators, with a different but

70

similarly exclusive prejudice, have preferred the miracle moms. Glance through any book used for religious education in grades first through twelfth and you'll generally find the stories of Eve, Sarah, Elizabeth and Mary—a rather sketchy way to connect the dots, biblically speaking. Hollywood's choice is understandable: The women who fit central casting's desire for a "babe" out front stay in the picture. The religion teacher's choice is regrettable in its limitations as well, since women with miraculously achieved births are not easy role models to follow.

Selecting other biblical women can make for spirited discussion in adult Bible study. For example, consider the prophetesses—nine of whom are mentioned in Scripture. Deborah, who exercises her office under the tree bearing her name, is a memorable wisdom figure. The general Barak refuses to take his army into battle unless she rides with him (see Judges 4-5). Moses' sister Miriam is a prophetess, and Isaiah refers to his own wife by that title—presumably not as a pet name. King Josiah defers to the prophetess Huldah when the book of the Law is recovered after the Exile. The king requires her word of authenticity before the book will be officially accepted (see 2 Kings 22 and 2 Chronicles 34). Five more women gifted with prophecy are noted in the New Testament.

We might also consider the women whose conspiracy to rescue Moses makes his illustrious career an option. First there are Shiphrah and Puah, the Hebrew midwives who defy Pharaoh's decree to kill all Hebrew males at birth. They risk their lives to save the future generation. Next come Moses' mother and his sister Miriam, who keep the baby at home as long as they dare and then watch over him at the water's edge. Pharaoh's daughter shows tremendous *chutzpah* (Hebrew for nerve) in adopting a clearly Hebrew baby, knowing her father's directives. These five women are responsible for seeing Moses to adulthood. Later, Moses' wife Zipporah, more aware of religious duty than her uninstructed mate, marks her sleeping husband with the blood from their young son's circumcision in order to save both males from the condemnation of the uncircumcised. Without these six women behind Moses, the nation would never have the chance to get behind *him* (see Exodus 2-4).

Other women are notable for their intelligence, virtue or wit. Rahab, a Moabite of Jericho, hands the Israelites their first great conquest in Canaan, revealing that she knows God's will in this matter (see Joshua 2). Tamar tricks her father-in-law Judah into fulfilling the Law when he refuses to do his duty as next of kin (for details, see Genesis 38). An Israelite girl, kidnapped as part of the booty of war, shows compassion for her foreign master who suffers from leprosy. She advises him to seek healing from a prophet in Israel, revealing a remarkable mercy for her oppressor. There is no indication that this kindness leads to her freedom (see 2 Kings 5). Abigail, the plucky wife of the fool Nabal, risks her life to save her husband from the consequences of his own mean-spiritedness when he refuses refreshment to David's soldiers. For her generosity and courage, David rewards her by sparing her household and later, after the death of her husband, inviting her to become one of his wives (see 1 Samuel 25). Although not much time is spent in chronicling the acts of women, the glimpses we get reveal an alertness and creativity that cannot be hidden beneath a woman's *burkha*.

Ruth, Judith and Esther

Women do not appear only as cameos in the Hebrew Scriptures, however; they are also the protagonists of their own tales in the books of Ruth, Judith and Esther. Although we don't know if women authored these books, or any part of the Bible for that matter, scholars suspect that details in Ruth and Judith (as well as parts of Samuel and Kings) indicate at least female collaboration in the forming of the tales. For example, reread the story of Hannah in 1 Samuel 1–2 or the story of the Shunammite woman in 2 Kings 4. Would a man include the tender details of Hannah bringing baby clothes to the shrine long after she gave up her son, or are these a mother's words? Or how about the Shunammite woman's proposal to establish a guest room for the prophet, and her husband's silence on the matter? This woman speaks like the head of her household. Likewise, reread the litany of furnishings she placed in the room. Are these not details only a hostess would be concerned with? Scholars raise these questions as an invitation to consider the role of women in the transmission of ancient stories.

Regardless of who authored these books, their content is unusual in that these stories concern the saving activity of women. The Book of Ruth, for example, is set in the time of the judges. A direct ancestor of King David (her great-grandson) and Jesus (see Matthew's lineage), Ruth is part of a long and significant line of marital decision making. A Moabite woman growing up outside of Israel, it is odd that she would figure in the story at all. Her mother-in-law Naomi is an Israelite, and both women have suffered the loss of their husbands due to famine. A third woman, Orpah, is widowed by Naomi's other son, and the three huddle together as Naomi resolves to go back to Israel, urging her young daughters-in-law to return to their fathers in the hopes they might marry again. Orpah departs— but Ruth stays. With some of the most passionate words ever uttered in Scripture, she insists her place is with Naomi: "Your people shall be my people, and your God my God" (Ruth 1:16). These words are heard at most Catholic weddings, but few recognize that they describe the bond between a daughter-in-law and her mother-in-law. Through Ruth's dedication to Naomi and trust in a God she did not know, Ruth becomes the wife of Boaz in Israel and takes her place in the genealogy of salvation.

Judith is the only woman in the Bible who is called a "savior." There is no other name to sum up this leader who is as holy, charismatic and courageous as anyone in the Hebrew story. When Israel is under attack by the Assyrian army, led by the dreaded General Holofernes, the elders panic and decide to surrender. Judith, hearing of this at her monastic estate, sends a stinging rebuke to the elders. Not only do they meekly accept this remonstrance from a widow but they also acknowledge her wisdom and ask for her prayers. Judith delivers far more than prayers. With her trusty maid as her only companion, Judith infiltrates the enemy camp and wines and dines with Holofernes himself. Once he is sufficiently inebriated, she decapitates him and hands the head to her maid, who drops it into her purse. Judith's return to her city is met with song and praise, not to mention proposals of marriage. She declines all offers, preferring to retire quietly, taking her faithful maid with her.

The Book of Esther describes another woman who rescues her people. Here, the action takes place among the Jews of the *diaspora*, those living outside of Israel. In the Persian Empire, things look bad for the children of Abraham because of the scheming Haman, who plots to massacre all the Israelites in a single day. Their only hope is Esther, adolescent Hebrew bride to the Persian king and new to his harem. Esther is no Judith: not pious or brave or even committed to the cause. Her uncle, Mordecai, twists her arm with emotional blackmail until she agrees to speak to the king on behalf of her race. Esther promptly faints in the king's presence out of fear of his displeasure, but the fainting spell only endears her to him more. Esther's lovely prayer for stamina, delivered before her audience with the king, is the only fragment of the book that makes it into the lectionary. Esther is read on the Thursday of the First Week of Lent—which is better than Judith, who is not included in the lectionary at all.

Women in the twenty-first century may find useful companions in these biblical personalities who are still waiting to take their rightful place in the story of salvation. When the timing is right and the Church is ready, these stories and others like them will at last be heard.

Questions for Reflection and Discussion

1. How many biblical women could you name before reading this chapter? Into which categories would you place these women: villainess, victim, miracle mom, or other? How has your impression of biblical women changed as a result of this review?

2. Name ten female villainesses or victims who have appeared on television, in film, or in songs. How do these stereotypes contribute to society's perception of women, especially in leadership roles?

3. Are miracle moms good to accentuate in religious education? Give reasons for your answer.

4. Among the Old Testament women with whom you are familiar, who is the most admirable and why?

5. With which of the three Hebrew books bearing women's names—Ruth, Judith and Esther—do you think would be useful for children or young people to become better acquainted? What values could these stories have for children of both sexes?

Prayer Activity

Consider women in the history of the Church or in our time who have made a significant contribution as Doctors of the Church (Catherine of Siena, Teresa of Avila, Thérèse of Lisieux) or founders of special works (Catherine McAuley of the Sisters of Mercy; Katherine Drexel, who championed education for children of color; Dorothy Day of the Catholic Worker; Catherine de Hueck Doherty of the interracial fellowship, Friendship House). Learn more about these women and others like them.

Wisdom, Proverbs, Sirach, Song of Songs
Ecclesiastes, Psalms, Job

Wisdom Asks
New Questions

For many people, traditional religion works just fine. The faith of their forebears isn't "broke," so don't fix it. To such people, religious truth is immutable and therefore expressions of that truth—in ritual, teaching and practice—should remain unchanged. But what happens when life events transpire to shake the unchanging truth we espouse? As hospice worker Rosemary Hubble notes in her book titled *Conversations on the Dung Heap: Reflections on Job,* nearly everyone feels betrayed by the sterility of static faith in the active phase of dying. The closer we get to our Maker, the more an unexamined understanding of God will no longer do. The truly religious questions arise in crisis: Is there a God? Is God just and merciful? Why do we suffer? How should we pray? What is the meaning of our lives? What will happen after death?

Some of us confront these questions long before dying. Loss, failure, disability and disappointment are little "deaths" that signal to us how fragile we are. In these events, the form of religion we have counted on all along may be unmasked as just another idol keeping us from the true God who waits beyond all our assumptions.

What Is Biblical Wisdom?

When we start asking the big religious questions, we enter the territory inhabited by the Wisdom tradition. Wisdom has many meanings in the Bible. First, it is an attribute of God made available to us if we seek it. Wisdom is often personified as a female who assisted God at the creation of the world and enlightens those who come to her (see Proverbs 8). Wisdom also refers to a body of literature grounded in human experience that espouses right living. Finally, Wisdom is a school of thought addressing the problem of human vulnerability in an immense and contradictory universe. Its roots lie in ancient cultures beyond Israel—Egypt, Mesopotamia, Greece—since the deepest questions that confound humanity are common to all people.

If the answers supplied by our religious upbringing sometimes seem inadequate in light of our experience, Wisdom writings offer some companionship. They ask questions rarely confronted in conventional religion and raise doubts regarding traditional answers. Wisdom literature lays bare the heartache of the human condition. How do we live in a world poised between goodness and evil, beauty and brutality, expansive possibility and the slamming of the door in death? The juxtaposition of limitless dreams and finite bodies is a kind of madness that requires intellectual satisfaction.

In the Wisdom school, it's okay to raise your hand and ask why. It's also acceptable to express pain, outrageous and uncertainty. If we cannot bring to God that which is real and deeply felt in our experience, then all we have left to offer is our false selves. Wisdom writers would suggest that much traditional piety has led us to do just that.

A New Tradition

The Law and the prophets were good enough for ancient Israel. Between the fixed principle of law and the dynamic proclamation of prophecy, the nation could readily plot its moral course. If Israel had been left undisturbed, its tradition may have remained majestically moored to these two core sources. But from the time of the kingdom's occupation by Assyria in the north and Babylon in the south, foreign influence moved from the periphery to the center of Israel's experience. Wanted or not, international ideas crept into the people's cultural awareness, and not all foreign influence was perceived negatively. When Cyrus of Persia released the Babylonian exiles a generation later to return to Judea, only a remnant went home. The rest decided that living and doing business in the bustling Orient wasn't half bad.

The Hebrew Wisdom tradition has its roots in this encounter with the East, as does the Apocalyptic worldview we hear in Daniel, Ezekiel, and books of the New Testament, especially Revelation. Both imports returned to Jerusalem and influenced later Jewish writers within Judea and in the *diaspora*, those Jews dispersed in other lands. Writings of this period not included in the Hebrew Scriptures were left out largely for this reason: They were written in Greek rather than Hebrew, evidence of foreign origins or influence. Therefore books like Tobit, Judith, Wisdom, Sirach, Baruch, Ezra, Nehemiah, Maccabees, and additions to Esther and Daniel, known only from Greek texts, lost credibility in the community of Israel for having taken shape in foreign lands.

The early church, living in the context of the diaspora itself after the first few generations, embraced these texts and included them in the Old Testament. Protestant reformers later removed them, but they remain as *Deuterocanonical* in the Catholic Bible, a "second canon" that is nonetheless divinely inspired.

What Does Wisdom Say?

The first thing we notice in Wisdom writings is what's missing in them. Considering that these books appear in the Bible, there is a remarkable absence of references to salvation history. Gone are the promises, the patriarchs, the Exodus, the Law, kings, priests and prophets for the most part. These key elements are not negated; they simply do not appear. With rare exceptions (see chapters 11–19 in the Book of Wisdom), Hebrew tradition is not the source of authority for Wisdom writers.

So what are the tenets of Wisdom? It's about LIFE—with capital letters—particularly how to attain the good life and what meaning one might glean from life's bitterness. What leads to the pleasures of long life, prosperity and prestige? Wisdom tradition points to two essential elements: right relationship with God and the exercise of self-control.

We may sigh when we consider this new religious simplification. Only these two things? A good relationship with God and discipline? It's a little like hearing the doctor tell us to eat right, get plenty of rest, and exercise. We know these things already (and continue to look for a magic pill to get around them). Perhaps the beginning of wisdom is when we stop resisting simple truths and begin to act on them.

Wisdom writers draw firm distinctions between the wise and the foolish, or the just and the wicked. But they are equally willing to sit with the mystery of suffering and refuse to dismiss it with easy rules of cause-and-effect as religion often has.

Wisdom writers are also willing to disagree with one another, or to offer counterpoints to the entire tradition. Is right relationship with God and self-control enough to ensure happiness? Talk to Job about that! Are the goals of wisdom—long life, prosperity and prestige—all they're cracked up to be? The writer of Ecclesiastes would argue that such things are dust in the wind. Although proverbs abound in Wisdom literature, one thing is clear: There are no easy answers to the complexity of existence.

Wisdom as Instructor

The best representatives of classic Wisdom literature are the books of Proverbs, Job, Ecclesiastes, Sirach and Wisdom. Scholars also include the Psalms, Song of Songs, Lamentation, Baruch, Tobit, Esther, Judith, and sometimes Jonah and Ruth in this category because they contain elements of the Wisdom worldview.

In the popular sense, human wisdom is an accumulation of tested teachings by sages. The Hebrew Wisdom school produced collections that fit into this category. Major sections of Proverbs and Sirach are composed of wise sayings such as: "Better is a dinner of vegetables where love is, than a fatted ox and hatred with it" (Proverbs 15:17) and "The idler is like the filth of dunghills; anyone that picks it up will shake it off his hand" (Sirach 22:2). Such sayings alert the hearer at once to the sort of action that is expected. Loving relationships trump prosperity. Wash your hands of idleness!

Tobit, Esther and Judith (and if you include them, Jonah and Ruth) are obviously not compilations of teachings. They are more like novellas, complete with heroes, tense plots, and high stakes. Unlike other Bible narratives, divine intervention is limited or imperceptible. (Jonah is an exception; surviving inside a fish is uncommon without heavenly aid.) Protagonists rely on their personal resources—faith, family ties, a sharp sword, fish guts, and street smarts—to make the outcome possible. The Wisdom tradition applauds such values and the underlying principle that we are actively—if not principally—responsible for what becomes of us.

Other Wisdom books, such as Ecclesiastes, Job, and the Psalms (the largest section of which is given over to laments), are not purely optimistic works that lead naturally to happy endings. They demonstrate the darker side of the Wisdom school, where God's ways are not so clear and innocent human suffering seems to be in conflict with the justice God has promised.

In Praise of Our Humanity

It may seem profane to speak of the human condition as "praiseworthy." Many of us have been taught to think: "Divine good, human bad." The evidence of original sin all around us can be so compelling that we may discount our humanity as morally bankrupt. God is good and worthy to be praised, and we—well, we prefer not to think about what we deserve.

Wisdom tradition takes a different approach. It celebrates the intrinsic goodness of our humanity. After all, God did once look upon creation and call it "very good." Although obscured by centuries of sin, the likeness of God remains imprinted on us. Wisdom trusts in that likeness and attempts to draw it forth in wise teaching. Most Wisdom teachers put their trust in God, yet they also have confidence in the potential for human beings to make wise choices.

This optimism is best demonstrated by the Song of Songs, a celebration of human sexual love. Most scholars today do not think it was written as an allegory about the relationship between God and Israel (nor, obviously, was it meant in the centuries before Christ to be an image of Jesus and the Church). Every text has an afterlife, as Carmelite scholar Father Roland Murphy admits, which assures us that an allegorical reading of the Song of Songs is not dishonest. Yet an absolute adherence to allegory denies us the beauty of its original meaning. Does it make us religious folks uncomfortable to delight in our sexuality and to imagine that God might have expected that when creating us as sexual beings?

The Song of Songs, incorporated into the Jewish, Catholic and Protestant canons of Scripture, is a testimony to the belief that human sexual love is holy. If we accept an allegorical "afterlife" interpretation as well, the text also affirms that sexual love is worthy to serve as an expression of God's love for us with all of its passion, fierce loyalty, mutuality, and unshakeable desire.

Lamentation

"When we hurt physically, we cry out in pain; when we hurt religiously, we lament," Franciscan scholar Father Michael Guinan explains in discussing the role of lamentation in the life of faith. The biblical lament is not so different from the contemporary one: Why this, O Lord? And for how long?

In somewhat less scholarly fashion, a friend of mine calls lamentation "religious whining." Any way you describe it, presenting a complaint to God was first perfected by Jeremiah, for whom another word for lamentation, *jeremiad*, was coined. Jeremiah lamented plenty in his own book, but the Book of Lamentations was attributed to him in deference to his mastery of the subject. (His scribe Baruch writes his own book more optimistically. Years with Jeremiah evidently failed to dampen his mood.) The Book of Lamentations has become a classic text for Holy Week, and the Man of Sorrows in chapter 3 has found his way into our hearts. After all, we too have drunk our own wormwood and forgotten, at times, what happiness is (see 3:15–17).

But when we think of first-class lamentation, nothing surpasses Psalm 22, which Jesus utters from the cross. "My God, my God, why have you forsaken me?" Here we experience the full wonder of the Wisdom tradition, which dares to hurl our pint-size human fury into the void that seems to separate us from God in times of anguish and injustice. What is God thinking? How could God let this happen? Wisdom literature may not always answer these questions, but it permits them to be asked, dignifying the struggle of every person who has ever dared to question in faith. In the tradition of lamentation, the psalmist finds renewed trust in God and hope for the future before the end. This reveals one thing more about the search for answers: A faith that dares to seek will find God at the end of every quest. A faith that dares not question, by comparison, risks missing the greatest encounter of all.

The Great Inquisitors

They come from opposite ends of the spectrum, the two great figures of Hebrew wisdom teaching. Job, the skid row champion, has a prosperous beginning but soon winds up in the back alley of life, the embodiment of grief and loss. By comparison, Qoheleth, the author of Ecclesiastes, is a slacker: idly successful, sitting atop his wealth and achievement, wondering if it's all been "a chasing after wind"(1:14). Yet together, these two guard the goalposts of Wisdom teaching. What is the meaning of human suffering, or worldly success for that matter? Does either circumstance reflect God's justice for those who experience them? If not, can meaning be assigned to human experience at all? Between Job and Qoheleth, one thing is sure: Religion isn't just for comfort anymore.

Job is a religious man. Not only that, he is also righteous in God's opinion, which counts for a lot. Still, he suffers every conceivable deprivation: financial ruin, the deaths of his children, the loss of his wife's support, illness, and—worst of all—the piety of friends who assign his losses to some unrepented, secret failure. Qoheleth, for his part, makes no pretense at piety. While not recommending folly, Qoheleth dismisses most Wisdom teaching as bogus. He attacks the incredibility of any religious idea that contradicts human experience.

Strangely enough, this puts Job and Qoheleth in the same camp—as two who reject the fundamental religious principle that God rewards the just and punishes the unjust through their circumstances. They haven't seen it. In fact, each in his own way has seen that life's rewards and punishments are dis-

83

turbingly arbitrary.

The inclusion of both works in the canon of Scripture reveals something hopeful for all of us. The suffering person can charge God with unfairness, regret being born, rage and lament, and still declare herself or himself a believer at the end of the day. Likewise, we can struggle with faith, never feel God's presence or be certain of the religious path, and still find ourselves represented among the inspired voices of Scripture. God seems more willing to honor disparate routes to truth than we are. Through his protests atop his dung heap, Job gets an audience with God at once. Qoheleth, we may presume, gets his by and by.

Life After Death?

When discussing Wisdom literature, the book known as the Wisdom of Solomon, or Wisdom for short, must round out the debate. Wisdom was the last book of the Old Testament to be written, just a generation before the birth of Jesus. As a late text, it tries to do it all: give counsel on right living, shed light on the mystery of suffering, and speak to the richness available to wisdom seekers. Unique in Wisdom literature, the second half of the book retells the story of salvation history from the perspective of Wisdom's own activity, erasing the names of the patriarchs as if they were insignificant actors compared to the role Wisdom played.

What makes the Book of Wisdom especially important is that it affirms the late-developing theology of the afterlife. In the century before Jesus, Jewish thought had begun to dabble in the possibility that there was more to death than just *sheol*— that shadowy underworld with no assigned seating, where the just and the unjust alike were deposited for all eternity. Souls in sheol endured a disembodied and static experience without hope of change. Residence in sheol could not be terminated because it was the very definition of human *terminus*, the final docking point of existence.

Within a century, the idea of afterlife did a flip so dramatic as to take on the force of a movement. The Pharisees of Jesus' time were already adamant believers in a final judgment with distinctive fates awaiting the just and the unjust. They also believed in the resurrection of the body and a vital afterlife experience, complete with angels and other spirits. This put them in opposition to the Temple orthodoxy, which dispelled this cosmology as so much bunk.

Since belief in an afterlife is absent through most of the Hebrew Scriptures, we search eagerly for the faint stirrings of that faith in the final books of the Old Testament. We find it in the Second Book of Maccabees, in the martyrs' story of the mother and her seven sons. As the third son holds out his hands to be cut off, he declares, "I got these from Heaven, and because of God's laws I disdain them, and from God I hope to get them back again" (7:11). His mother also shows trust in a bodily resurrection when she encourages her sons to endure: "[God] will in mercy give life and breath back to you again, since you now forget yourselves for the sake of God's laws" (7:23). An amazing statement for a mother to make, certainly— but more astonishing still in light of a tradition that never dreamed even its patriarchs would merit better than sheol in the end.

Later, in 2 Maccabees 12:42–46, Judas Maccabeus makes theological history by praying for the dead soldiers under his command. In doing so, he affirms the afterlife as a situation that is distinctive, personal and changeable, dealing yet another blow to the image of static sheol.

In the Book of Wisdom, the Old Testament exposition of afterlife reaches its apex. "The souls of the righteous are in the hand of God, and no torment will ever touch them…. Their hope is full of immortality" (3:1, 4). Chapter 3 of the Book of Wisdom has become standard at Catholic funerals because of its confident hope in the fate of the just after death. When death has lost its sting, salvation achieves its ultimate expression.

Questions for Reflection and Discussion

1. When have you been challenged to let your religious beliefs grow or change due to life experiences that didn't "fit" the old mold? What adjustments did you make?

85

2. Are there things you might say to a human being that you would be uncomfortable saying to God? Does refraining from saying these things make your relationship with God less real? Explain your answer.

3. Choose one psalm that particularly appeals to you. Describe the features of the psalm and why they speak to you personally.

4. Which aspects of the Wisdom tradition are most important to you, for example, its affirmation of human choice and experience, its freedom to question established beliefs?

5. Imagine you are in charge of establishing the canon of Scripture and all the choices have been made except for the Wisdom books. Which ones are "in" your canon for sure? Are there any you might leave out if the final vote were yours? Explain why.

Prayer Activity

Resolve to have an honest relationship with God. Present the full contents of your heart in prayer, complete with warts, jealousies, sadness, disappointment and anger. Dare to relate to God without pretending. And pray for the dead, especially those who have been given to you to love.

Afterword

The Challenge of the Hebrew Scriptures

The God of the Hebrew Scriptures is a wild and mysterious deity. Which is to say, human beings came to an awareness of God through those aspects of our world—and ourselves—that are wild and mysterious. The stories of these encounters were recorded so that future generations might come to know the God who creates and promises and saves.

The Hebrew story suggests that God is not yet finished with us. Original creation may have taken six days, but on the seventh day the Creator merely rested. There is no evidence that God retired altogether. Instead, after a pause, God took up the work of co-creation with us, creatures invested with the divine capacity for freedom and choice. And so the world continues to evolve, no longer simply through natural forces imbued with the divine command but also under human influence and decree. Every decision we make is part of that evolution. What you and I do matters in ultimate ways.

It would be an oversimplification to boil down the Bible to one message. Scripture is a full orchestra sounding major and minor keys, admitting motifs of many kinds into the whole. Is one motif truer than another? Can any one of them be true alone? We would be poorer to insist on that. But surely the underlying premise of every book of Scripture is that God created us to choose. Sometimes the choice is laid out explicitly, as Moses did in the desert: "I call heaven and earth to witness against you today that I have set before you life and death, blessings and curses. Choose life so that you and your descendants may live, loving the Lord your God, obeying him, and holding fast to him..." (Deuteronomy 30:19–20). At other times, the choice is implicit in the opposing tensions of daily living. But choose we must. In relationships, events, and especially moments of challenge and temptation, we must decide which way we are headed. Are we moving toward life, as Moses recommends? Or are we going in the general direction of destruction?

Our present society values autonomy as a divine right and a national birthright. And yet we make so many perilous choices against the cause of life with our freedom that we are drifting toward death with every act of violence and greed, with our wars and our indifference to the plight of others. Hebrew biblical tradition, with its Law, prophets and Wisdom, speaks in opposition to our course. Creation cries out as she suffers the consequences of what we do. We are making dangerous choices, and in the direction we are headed we are the most endangered species of all.

Yet for all our talk of freedom, many in our society experience themselves as helpless. Friends and family members are paralyzed by insecurity, anxiety and depression in increasing numbers. Our autonomy seems to be an illusion as we trudge through our routines and slide down the chute of predestination: to this school or trade, along this career path, or into this foreordained relationship. We grow up conditioned to a particular domestic pattern of neglect, abuse or conflict and seem fated to it. Our family of origin becomes the mirror of our destiny, and we don't know how to escape it. The sins of the fathers and mothers are visited on the next generation as we passively assent to them, and we become the people they were without reflection.

The most common report I hear from unhappy people is: "I can't help it. This is who I am. It's in my genes. It's the way I was raised. It's all I know. It's the way the world is." This way of thinking could be the biggest and most life-threatening lie of all. The worst the Great Deceiver can do is to hide from us the reality of our freedom. If God created us in the divine image, then we are fundamentally creative beings as well. And if we do not exercise the tremendous gift of our creativity in free choices, then yes, we can expect to be anxious and depressed like animals in a cage. We will have suffocated the divine word that cries out within us and demands a hearing.

The Hebrew Scriptures challenge us to embrace a different destiny and to choose life in all of its wild mystery and opportunity. God calls us out of a leaden existence of passivity and into the dynamic exercise of responsibility for who we are and for what happens next. Will we be faithful to this stewardship and risk the freedom of the children of God? If we choose otherwise, we have no one to blame but ourselves. However, should we choose to be faithful, nothing could be more thrilling and hopeful.

Peace be with you on this journey.

Appendices

Selected Resources

General Bible Tools
These basic books belong on the bookshelf of every serious student of the Bible.

The New American Bible (National Council of Catholic Bishops)
The Revised Standard Version Bible (National Council of the Churches of Christ in the U.S.A.)
The New World Dictionary-Concordance to the New American Bible (World Book Publishing)
NRSV Exhaustive Concordance (Thomas Nelson Publishers)
The New Jerome Bible Handbook (Liturgical Press)
Dictionary of the Bible (Simon and Schuster)

Commentaries for Lectionary-Based Scripture Study
The following three resources are for those interested in Bible study in conjunction with the Scripture readings used at Mass. The first two titles follow the Sunday readings. The third title is for those who want to reflect on the daily Mass readings. All are available from Bayard/Twenty-Third Publications.

Alice Camille. *God's Word Is Alive! Entering the Sunday Readings*
——. " Exploring the Sunday Readings." Serial publication mailed monthly
Paul Boudreau. *Between Sundays: Daily Gospel Reflections and Prayers*

Recommended Scripture Videos
For accuracy, breadth and beauty, I highly recommend only one Bible video series. All of the following films are from "The Bible Collection," Turner Home Entertainment series, currently on VHS format, available from Vision Video at www.catholic video.com.

Abraham. Featuring Richard Harris and Barbara Hershey. 150 mins.

Jacob. Featuring Matthew Modine, Lara Flynn Boyle, Irene Papas. 94 mins.

Joseph. Featuring Paul Mercurio, Ben Kingsley, Martin Landau, Lesley Ann Warren. 185 mins.

Moses. Featuring Ben Kingsley, Frank Langella, Christopher Lee. 184 mins.

Samson and Delilah. Featuring Eric Thal, Dennis Hopper, Elizabeth Hurley. 182 mins.

David. Featuring Nathaniel Parker, Leonard Nimoy, Jonathan Price, Sheryl Lee. 180 mins.

Special Topics

Edith Deen. *All of the Women of the Bible* (New York: Harper and Row)

John Endres, SJ. *Temple, Monarchy, and Word of God* (Collegeville, MN: Michael Glazier)

Carlo Maria Martini. *A Prophetic Voice in the City: Meditations on the Prophet Jeremiah* (Collegeville, MN: Liturgical Press)

Eileen Schuller. *Post-Exilic Prophets* (Collegeville, MN: Michael Glazier)

Carmel McCarthy, RSM and William Riley. *The Old Testament Short Story: Explorations into Narrative Spirituality* (Collegeville, MN: Michael Glazier)

Daniel J. Harrington, SJ. *The Maccabean Revolt* (Collegeville, MN: Michael Glazier)

Old Testament Books of the Bible

The following is a list of books of the Hebrew Scriptures as they are categorized by the Jewish community who wrote them. I include notes about Catholic and Protestant variations in name and category. All of the books below are included in the Catholic Bible.

Pentateuch (The Law)
These five books are also known as the Books of Moses.
Genesis
Exodus
Leviticus
Numbers
Deuteronomy

Former Prophets
These are included in the Catholic Bible under the Historical Books.
Joshua
Judges
1, 2 Samuel (old 1, 2 Kings)
1, 2 Kings (old 3, 4 Kings)

Major and Minor Prophets
The first three are Major Prophets; the rest are Minor Prophets.
Isaiah
Jeremiah
Ezekiel
Hosea
Joel
Amos
Obadiah
Micah
Nahum

Habakkuk
Zephaniah
Haggai
Zechariah
Malachi
Jonah

The Writings
The Jewish Bible is composed of Law, Writings and Prophets. Catholic Bibles tend to divide the Writings, Former Prophets, and Deuterocanonical Books into Historical and Wisdom Books. The seven Wisdom Books appear with an asterisk.

Psalms*
Job*
Proverbs*
Ruth
Song of Songs* (old Canticle of Canticles)
Ecclesiastes*
Lamentations
Esther
Daniel
Ezra (old 1 Esdras)
Nehemiah (old 2 Esdras)
1, 2 Chronicles (old 1, 2 Paralipomenon)

Deuterocanonical
These books have limited acceptance in the Jewish community, and most Protestants do not accept these books as canonical. Some Protestant Bibles include them separately under the name "Apocrypha."

Tobit
Judith
Wisdom*
Sirach* (Ecclesiasticus)
Baruch
1, 2 Maccabees
Additions to Daniel and Esther

How Old Testament Events Fit into Larger World History

You rarely find such lists in either Scripture or secular resources, because establishing such time frames is risky business. Science and biblical scholarship keep making advances, and these numbers can be out of date within a short period of time. As ballpark frameworks, however, these kinds of time lines can help us gain perspective on the place of the Hebrew story in the larger story of history.

5 billion years ago	Origin of the earth
550 million B.C.	Origin of plants and animals
600,000 B.C.	Human life emerges
3200 B.C.	Stone Age
3200–2050 B.C.	Early Bronze Age
2050–1550 B.C.	Middle Bronze Age: Kingdoms of Egypt, Assyria, Babylon on the rise Age of the Patriarchs: Noah, Abraham, Isaac, Jacob, Joseph
1500–1300 B.C.	Hebrew slavery in Egypt
1300–1225 B.C.	Moses and the Exodus
1225–1200 B.C.	Joshua conquers Canaan
1200–1050 B.C.	The Judges: Gideon, Deborah, Jephthah, Samson
1020–587 B.C.	The Monarchy: Saul, David, Solomon. Temple built in Jerusalem
932 B.C.	Kingdom divided into Israel (North) and Judah (South)
722 B.C.	Fall of Samaria (capitol of Israel) to Assyria
587 B.C.	Fall of Jerusalem (capitol of Judah) to Babylonia

538 B.C.	Exile ends. Faithful remnant restored. Second Temple is built
63 B.C.	Roman rule begins

The Prophets
in the Context
of the Hebrew Story

The two early prophets have no surviving works to their credit, if they wrote at all. The three Major and twelve Minor Prophets of the classical period each left a book to his name. (Some, like Isaiah, left three, if you count the work of followers in subsequent generations.) The positioning of each prophet—as pre-exilic, post-exilic, or in Babylon—is significant to his message. Although Scripture scholars do not always agree on the dating of the prophets, these are majority votes at the moment, subject to further scholarship.

932 B.C.	Kingdom divides after Solomon's death into Israel (to the north, with its capitol in Samaria) and Judah (to the south, with Jerusalem as its capitol)
900–800 B.C.	The early prophets: Elijah and Elisha (prophets to Israel)
760–740 B.C.	First writing prophets: Amos and Hosea (prophets to Israel); Isaiah and Micah (prophets to Judah)
722 B.C.	Fall of Samaria, capitol of Israel
640–587 B.C.	All subsequent prophets are to the remaining southern kingdom: Zephaniah, Nahum, Habakkuk, Jeremiah
587 B.C.	Fall of Jerusalem, capitol of Judah; exile to Babylon; prophets of the Babylonian Exile: Ezekiel, Deutero-Isaiah
538 B.C.	Exile ends and remnant returns to Jerusalem
520–300 B.C.	Post-exilic prophets: Haggai, Zechariah, Malachi, Trito-Isaiah, Obadiah, Jonah, Joel, Daniel

Wisdom Writings

The classification of these books is quite loose. Only Proverbs, Job, Ecclesiastes, Sirach and the Book of Wisdom are considered classic Wisdom literature. The other books derive in some part from the tradition, although they contain other elements as well. Dating is very imprecise because the nature of the books is non-historical, and there are few narratives that reflect historical events. Jonah is a "floater," more naturally included in the prophetic tradition.

c. 587 B.C.	Lamentations
c. 550–450 B.C.	Proverbs
Post-exilic	Song of Songs, Job
c. 400s B.C.	Esther (the original manuscript with later Greek additions in the second century, as it appears in most Catholic Bibles)
c. 300 B.C.	Baruch (with earlier sections dating perhaps to 597 B.C.)
c. 200s B.C.	Ecclesiastes
c. 200s B.C.-10 A.D.	Psalms (in various languages and versions up to final Jewish text)
200–180 B.C.	Tobit
c. 180 B.C.	Sirach
c. 100–50 B.C.	Judith
c. 50 B.C.	Wisdom (last book of the Hebrew Scriptures)

Jonah, if included in Wisdom literature, has been dated variously between 520 and 200 B.C.

Important Dates in the Formation of the Bible as We Have It Today

c. 1200–700 B.C.	Stories of Pentateuch and Samuel/Kings taking shape
c. 800 B.C.	Books of prophecy begun
c. 500 B.C.	Collection of Pentateuch completed
c. 300 B.C.	Prophetic books end
c. 200 B.C.–0	Most Wisdom literature composed
100 A.D.	Jewish community establishes its canon
382–405	Jerome, great church Scripture scholar, compiles standard translation of the Bible in Latin (known as the Vulgate)
1228	Stephen Langton, Archbishop of Paris, adds chapter numbers to the Bible
c. 1455	Johann Gutenberg prints first mass-produced Bibles, taking the Bible from the monasteries to the literate everywhere
1545–1563	Council of Trent establishes complete canon of Scripture
1555	Robert Etienne fixes numbering of Bible verses
1609–1763	Douay-Rheims translation and revision from the Vulgate for Catholic use in English (King James Version produced in 1611)
1943	Pope Pius XII, in *Divino Afflante Spiritu,* considers the role of culture in shaping and interpreting Scripture
1947–1956	Dead Sea Scrolls transform modern biblical scholarship
1965	Vatican II, *Dogmatic Constitution on Divine Revelation,* encourages our contemporary understanding of Scripture

Also from ACTA Publications

Invitation to the New Testament
A Catholic Approach to the Christian Scriptures
Alice Camille

A companion to *Invitation to the Old Testament,* providing an overview of the entire New Testament through the lens of Catholic tradition and teaching. (112-page softcover, $9.95)

Invitation to Catholicism
Beliefs + Teachings + Practices
Alice Camille

Everyone from lifelong Catholics to interested non-Catholics will welcome the easy-to-understand, logical explanations found in this overview of Catholic beliefs, teachings and practices. (240-page softcover, $9.95)

Getting to Know the Bible
An Introduction to Sacred Scripture for Catholics
Rev. Melvin L. Farrell, SS
revised by Joseph McHugh

A clear, concise overview of the entire Bible for Catholics, offering an introduction to all the major books of Scripture, from Genesis through Revelation. (112-page softcover, $6.95)

The Rosary
Mysteries of Joy, Light, Sorrow and Glory
Alice Camille

New reflections on each of the mysteries of the Rosary, including the new Mysteries of Light, with a concise history of the Rosary and reflections on its meaning for the new millennium. (112-page softcover, $6.95)

Life in Christ
A Catholic Catechism for Adults
Revs. Gerard Weber and James Killgallon

This bestselling catechism for adults presents all aspects of Catholic teaching in a question-and-answer format that is easy to use yet thorough and comprehensive. (327-page softcover, $6.95)

Available from booksellers or call 800-397-2282
www.actapublications.com